SPIRITUAL GIFTS

Finding Your Position on Team Jesus!

REALFAITH.COM

By Mark Driscoll

Spiritual Gifts: Finding Your Position on Team Jesus!
© 2021 by Mark Driscoll

ISBN: 978-1-7374103-1-7 (Paperback)
ISBN: 978-1-7374103-2-4 (E-book)

CONTENTS

REAL GROUPS
WITH REAL FAITH

Faith that does not result in good deeds is not real faith.
James 2:20, TLB

At Real Faith, we believe that the Word of God isn't just for us to read, it's to be obeyed. And living in community with fellow believers is one of the ways God the Father allows us to learn and grow to become more like His Son Jesus through the power of the Holy Spirit. We do this through something called Real Groups. Here are a few tips to start your own.

1. Invite
Invite your friends, neighbors, family, coworkers, and enemies, because they all need Jesus whether they know Him or not! Whether it's a group of men, women, families, students, or singles, explain that you'd like to start a weekly sermon-based small group based on Pastor Mark Driscoll's sermons.

2. Listen to the sermon on realfaith.com or on the Real Faith app
You can host a viewing party to watch Real Faith Live and discuss it all at once, or you can watch it separately and gather to discuss it at another time that works for the group.

3. Get into God's Word
In addition to watching the sermon, make sure you and all group members have a study guide from realfaith.com for the current sermon series. There are questions for personal reflection as well as for groups that can guide your devotional times throughout the week. You can also sign up for Daily Devos at realfaith.com.

4. Gather together

Whether at someone's house, a public place, or through something like Zoom, meet weekly to discuss the sermon and what God has taught you through it. The great thing about Real Groups is that you don't all have to be in the same location. You can talk about sermon takeaways, what stood out to you in the study guide, or what God taught you in His Word that week. Focus on personal application as much as possible.

5. Pray

When you gather, feel free to share prayer requests, pray for each other on the spot, and continue praying throughout the week. Prayer is a great unifying force that God gives us to strengthen His family.

6. Share

Send us photos, videos, testimonies, and updates of how your group is doing to hello@realfaith.com. You might even be featured on our Real Faith Live show!

There are plenty more resources to discover at **realfaith.com/real-groups**, as well. We will be praying for you and your group and look forward to hearing what God does through it.

PREFACE: WELCOME TO TEAM JESUS!

In the earliest days of the Christian Church, there were two groups of people in the vast and powerful Roman Empire.

The powerful majority of people would publicly proclaim "Caesar is Lord". In doing so, they were declaring that their ultimate allegiance, above everyone and everything else, was to the ruler of their nation.

The persecuted minority of people would publicly proclaim, "Jesus is Lord". In doing so, they were practicing godly civil disobedience by declaring that their ultimate allegiance above everyone and everything else was the King of their Kingdom.

God is referred to as "Lord" thousands of times in the Old Testament. Jesus changed world history referring to Himself as "Lord" on multiple occasions.[a] To this day, Jesus stands alone in world history as the only founder of any major world religion to declare himself as God and Lord.

Echoing Christ, throughout the gospels, which serve as the most detailed historical record of Jesus' earthly life, death, burial, resurrection, and ascension numerous people refer to Jesus as "Lord", a title that He receives gladly. Examples include a blind man[b] and two blind men[c], Peter[d], a leper[e], a centurion soldier[f], a woman caught in adultery[g], Martha[h], Mary[i], John[k], and the disciples[m], among others. In some form or fashion, every New Testament book refers to Jesus Christ as Lord, often simply calling Him the "Lord Jesus Christ". For early Christians, the shortest summary of their commitment and conviction was simply, "Jesus Christ is Lord".[n]

---

[a] Matthew 4:7, 4:10-11; Luke 4:8, 4:12; Acts 9:5, 22:8, 26:15 [b] Matthew 9:28 [c] Matthew 20:30 [d] Matthew 7:14; Luke 5:8, 20:30; John 12:36, 21:15, 21:17 [e] Luke 5:12 [f] Luke 7:6 [g] John 8:11 [h] John 11:21,39 [i] John 11:32 [k] John 13:25, 21:7, 21:20-21 [m] John 21:12 [n] Philippians 2:11

Team Jesus

Is Jesus Christ your Lord?

If Jesus Christ is your Lord, then you are on Team Jesus!

Team Jesus includes all of the born-again believers from all of the nations, cultures, and languages of the world throughout human history in what theologians call the universal Church. Included on Team Jesus are all the Christian denominations, networks, teams, tribes, and traditions along with all ministries and followers of Christ doing Christian ministry in what theologians call the local church.

Since we all have the same Lord, we are on the same team. This little concept has big implications. We've all been on some kind of team. There are project teams in school called work groups, sports teams, military teams called units, college teams called clubs, work teams called departments, political teams called parties, and Christian teams called ministries. For any team to thrive, every person on the team needs to follow the team leader, discover their role or position on the team, accept that assignment, and do their best to grow in doing it as well as they possibly can. The same is true for Team Jesus. My hope and prayer in this project that includes this book, along with free sermons and daily devotions at realfaith.com, is to help you find your position on Team Jesus.

For some, this discovery process will result in finding a place to serve in your existing church or ministry so that you are getting out of the stands and onto the field. For others, this discovery process will result in finding a new place to serve in church or ministry that is new to you. Sadly, sometimes people see Christians moving from one church to another as a bad thing. Often, this is a good thing, as our Lord moves people from one place to another because their unique contribution is needed elsewhere. Since we are all on the same team, this is often a good thing.

For example, in Acts 13:1-3 we read, "Now there were in the church at Antioch prophets and teachers, Barnabas, Simeon who was called Niger, Lucius of Cyrene, Manaen a lifelong friend of Herod the tetrarch, and Saul. While they were worshiping the Lord and fasting, the Holy Spirit said, 'Set apart for me Barnabas and Saul for the work to which I have called them.' Then after fasting and praying they laid their hands on them and sent them off." The early church at Antioch had an incredible preaching team – a multiracial pulpit with five anointed Bible teachers that included Barnabas the encourager and Paul the Apostle. In basketball, this would be like having 5 Hall of Fame shooting guards on one team. What does God do? The Holy

Spirit gives a revelation to the church leaders that the two most well-known preachers, Barnabas and Saul (or Paul), should be sent out to do ministry elsewhere.

Rather than having five incredible preachers at one church, God the Holy Spirit wanted to spread them out among multiple churches. Practically, this makes sense. If one soccer team has five goalies but no shooter, and another team has five shooters but no goalie, swapping team members strengthens both teams. God does this all the time. Since our Lord is the coach of Team Jesus, He not only decides which position we play but also has the full right to put us wherever He wants and move us around as needed. At Real Faith, we are praying that God

Being Spirit-empowered does not mean we are equal to Jesus, but it does mean we can do some of what He did by the Spirit's power.

uses this study to help you find your position on Team Jesus because your contribution is needed. God has uniquely prepared you to find your purpose and pursue it with passion to continue the Spirit-filled ministry of Christ as a Christian, which we will learn next.

CHAPTER 1
THE SPIRIT-FILLED MINISTRY OF CHRIST AND CHRISTIANS

1 Corinthians 12:7 – To each is given the manifestation of the Spirit for the common good.

My mom and dad got married and had me, the first of five kids, at a young age. Like Jesus, my dad was named Joseph and worked a job swinging a hammer to feed his family. My dad worked tirelessly to provide for our family, working long hard hours during the week, and working even more on side jobs during the weekend.

Growing up, I admired my dad's work ethic driven by his love for our family. When I was a young boy, I can still remember the first time he took me to work with him. Like my dad, I wore jeans, a white tee shirt, and work boots. My mom packed my little lunch box and filled my little thermos just like my dad. I even had a little hard hat and some tools to carry to the truck, determined to be a helpful crewmember to my pops.

On the job, my dad gave me a few simple chores like picking up scraps of wood, and let me drive a few nails, among other things. At the time, I thought I was being a big help to my dad. Looking back, my dad did not bring me to work with him because he needed me, but because he loved me. He could have done the job easily, even more easily, without me. Pops wanted me to see him at work and for us to spend time together to build our relationship.

God is a Father, and you are His child. Doing ministry is simply going to work with your Dad. Jesus Christ, the Son of the Father and your Big Brother, explains ministry this very way repeatedly, especially in the gospel of John:

·John 5:17 – Jesus answered them, "My Father is working until now, and I am working."

·John 5:36 – "...the works that the Father has given me to accomplish, the very works that I [Jesus] am doing..."

·John 10:32 – Jesus answered them, "I have shown you many good works from the Father..."

·John 10:38 – "...believe the works, that you may know and understand that the Father is in me [Jesus] and I am in the Father."

·John 14:10–17 – "Do you not believe that I [Jesus] am in the Father and the Father is in me? The words that I say to you I do not speak on my own authority, but the Father who dwells in me does his works. Believe me that I am in the Father and the Father is in me, or else believe on account of the works themselves. Truly, truly, I say to you, whoever believes in me will also do the works that I do; and greater works than these will he do, because I am going to the Father. Whatever you ask in my name, this I will do, that the Father may be glorified in the Son. If you ask me anything in my name, I will do it. If you love me, you will keep my commandments. And I will ask the Father, and he will give you another Helper, to be with you forever, even the Spirit of truth, whom the world cannot receive, because it neither sees him nor knows him. You know him, for he dwells with you and will be in you."

Jesus Christ did His ministry, which was the work the Father assigned to Him by the power of the Holy Spirit, and promised that the Father's work would continue through the rest of His sons and daughters. How is this possible? By being Spirit-filled like Jesus.

Spirit-Filled Jesus

What does it mean to be Spirit-empowered in the truest sense of the word? It means to be like Jesus![a]

Sadly, most of the ancient Christian creeds, which are vital to orthodox theology, repeatedly miss out on Jesus' life. They say He was born, He died, then rose. But what else did He do? We must focus on what is missing from the creeds – the Spirit-empowered life of Jesus. I wrote an entire book on this called *Spirit-Filled Jesus*, but a summary will suffice to establish Jesus Christ as our perfect example for using spiritual gifts for Spirit-filled ministry.

How did Jesus live His sinless life and die on the cross for our sin? Most Christians would answer simply, "He was God." And yes, there is a sense in which this is true. Jesus is eternally God – past, present, and future. However, in the greatest act of humility the world has ever known, Jesus joined His divinity to humanity, taking the form of a servant, and temporarily set aside the continual use of His divine attributes.[b] Simply put, this means that Jesus did not cheat

---

[a] John 6:63; Romans 8:5-8; Galatians 5:22-23; 1 John 5:11-12   [b] Philippians 2:1-7

while on the earth and lean into His deity to make His hard times easy. Hebrews 4:15 says, "We do not have a high priest who is unable to sympathize with our weaknesses, but one who, in every respect, has been tempted as we are, yet without sin."

If Jesus chose to lay down the use of His divine rights, how was He able to live the perfect life He lived? How did Jesus resist temptation? How did Jesus forgive His enemies? How did Jesus remain obedient even to the point of death on the cross? How did Jesus perform miracles? How did Jesus preach? How did Jesus endure suffering? How did Jesus obey? How did Jesus heal? How did Jesus cast out demons? It was all by the power of the Holy Spirit! He was Spirit-filled, Spirit-anointed, and Spirit-led. As Peter said in Acts 10:38, "God anointed Jesus of Nazareth with the Holy Spirit and with power. He went about doing good and healing all who were oppressed by the devil, for God was with him."

Jesus' life was lived, fully human, by the power of the Holy Spirit. Too often, when we think about the role of the Holy Spirit, we turn just to the book of Acts to see how the Holy Spirit empowers believers. But Acts is a sequel to the book of Luke. For Luke, the words "power" and "Holy Spirit" are almost always interchangeable, both in his Gospel and in Acts.[a]

The book of Luke is the account of the Spirit-empowered ministry of Christ, and Acts is the account of the Spirit-empowered ministry of Christians. Christian ministry is an extension of Christ's ministry through His people by the Spirit's power. Jesus' life by the Spirit's empowerment is repeatedly stressed in Luke's Gospel. We find, for example, that Jesus was conceived by the Holy Spirit and given the title "Christ", which means "anointed [by the Holy Spirit]". Jesus baptized people with the Holy Spirit, and the Holy Spirit descended upon Jesus at His own baptism. Furthermore, Jesus was "full of the Holy Spirit" and "led by the Spirit"; He came "in the power of the Spirit" and declared that "the Spirit of the Lord is upon me". He also "rejoiced in the Holy Spirit". Regarding the Holy Spirit's ministry to and through Christians, Jesus also promised that God the Father would "give the Holy Spirit to those who ask him" and that the Holy Spirit would teach us once He was sent.[b]

Spirit-Filled Christian Ministry

In John 14:15-27 and 16:7-14, Jesus said it was "to our advantage" that He

---

[a] We can see this by looking at the words of Jesus in Luke 24 and then in Acts 1:8. In light of that, Luke 5:17; 6:19; and 8:46 also speak loudly. [b] See Luke 1–2; 3:16, 21-22; 4:1-2, 14, 18; 10:21; 11:13; 12:12; cf. Isaiah 61:1

would no longer be with us on the earth, because in His absence, He would send a "Helper," the Spirit of truth, to be with us and to lead us into all truth. He said the Father would send the Spirit in Jesus' name to teach us all things and bring into remembrance all that He said. Jesus said the Spirit would convict the world concerning sin, righteousness, and judgement. In possibly the greatest promise of the coming work of the Spirit, Jesus said the Spirit would take everything that is Jesus' and make it known to us. All these promises were fulfilled when the Holy Spirit was poured out on all believers in Jesus Christ at the Pentecost[a] and the subsequent outpourings of the Spirit recorded in the book of Acts.[b]

Being Spirit-empowered does not mean we are equal to Jesus, but it does mean we can do some of what He did by the Spirit's power. Let me make this very clear and simple: by the power of the Holy Spirit, you can overcome the temptation to sin, you can become more like Jesus Christ, you can understand and apply Scripture, you can pray over the sick and not be shocked if/when some are healed, you can pray with those experiencing demonic torment and see deliverance, you can have a joy that does not come from the circumstances around you but from the Spirit within you, and you can expect to see lost people saved, saved people grow, and inbreaking and outpouring of the Kingdom of God scattered throughout the otherwise mundane days of your life.

Being Spirit-empowered like Jesus means living on mission in culture doing ministry to establish the church and expand the Kingdom as Jesus did. It's not about expanding your own kingdom. It's not about you at all. It's all about Jesus. It's all about Jesus' mission to seek and save sinners. That's what it means to be Spirit-empowered –saved by Jesus and sent on mission, empowered by the Spirit to serve Team Jesus!

What we see in Acts is that Jesus' people – the church – continue His ministry by the power of the Holy Spirit and through the outpouring and filling of the Spirit. Much of the Spirit's work is missional: making disciples and planting churches. This is not because that is the church's mission; rather, it is the Spirit's mission, and the church is merely part of it.

Acts records what happens when the Church follows the Spirit. Acts is often wrongly called the Acts of the Apostles. The truth is it's the Acts of the Holy Spirit. He is the driving force of the mission of the Church and does extraordinary things through ordinary people. This gives us hope that He can use us to advance the mission of Jesus as we find our position and do our part on Team Jesus!

---

[a] Acts 2 [b] Acts 8, 10-11, 19

Spiritual Gifts

Spiritual gifts are any ministry abilities empowered by God the Holy Spirit. In the New Testament, spiritual gifts are spoken of in the original Greek text as "*pneumatikon*" and "*charisma*" or "*charismata*". The former refers to the work of the Spirit in and through a person. The latter refers to the grace of God flowing in and through a believer and is also the origin of the word "charismatic" that is commonly used to describe Christians. Therefore, a spiritual gift is the ability to have God's grace work for you, in you, and through you by the power of the Holy Spirit.

In the New Testament, there are four lists of spiritual gifts:

·1 Corinthians 12:8–11,28 – For to one is given through the Spirit the utterance of wisdom, and to another the utterance of knowledge according to the same Spirit, to another faith by the same Spirit, to another gifts of healing by the one Spirit, to another the working of miracles, to another prophecy, to another the ability to distinguish between spirits, to another various kinds of tongues, to another the interpretation of tongues. All these are empowered by one and the same Spirit, who apportions to each one individually as he wills...And God has appointed in the church first apostles, second prophets, third teachers, then miracles, then gifts of healing, helping, administrating, and various kinds of tongues.

·Romans 12:6–8 – Having gifts that differ according to the grace given to us, let us use them: if prophecy, in proportion to our faith; if service, in our serving; the one who teaches, in his teaching; the one who exhorts, in his exhortation; the one who contributes, in generosity; the one who leads, with zeal; the one who does acts of mercy, with cheerfulness.

·Ephesians 4:11-12 – And he gave the apostles, the prophets, the evangelists, the shepherds and teachers, to equip the saints for the work of ministry, for building up the body of Christ...

·1 Peter 4:10-11 – As each has received a gift, use it to serve one another, as good stewards of God's varied grace: whoever speaks, as one who speaks oracles of God; whoever serves, as one who serves by the strength that God supplies—in order that in everything God may be glorified through Jesus Christ.

None of these lists is the same, which has led some people to conclude that, by combining all the lists, we can arrive at the full list of spiritual gifts. More likely, these spiritual gifts lists are examples and not exhaustive. For example, leading worship is not listed as a spiritual gift, but it is self-evident that this is best done by a person gifted by and filled with the Spirit. Paul also spoke of his celibacy as a "gift" not mentioned elsewhere in Scripture but given to him by God to aid the difficult life of ministry travel he was called to.[a]

Furthermore, Spirit-empowered ministry also occurred in the Old Testament for a variety of purposes, including the construction of the Temple: "the Spirit's activity was largely exclusive to God's people, Israel, and generally in the form of either empowerment for a specific task, and/or revelation of God's will. For example, the Spirit worked among the artisans for the garments of the priests and elements of the tabernacle in the exodus narrative (Exod 28:3; 31:3; 35:31; Turner, Spiritual Gifts, 4). The Spirit was also active among Israel's chosen leaders, including Moses and the 70 elders during Israel's wilderness wanderings (Num 11:16–17, 24–29), the judges (Judg 3:10; 6:34; 11:29; 14:6, 19; 15:14–15), and the kings (1 Sam 10:1–11; 16:13; 19:20). Alongside Israel's leadership, the prophets are likewise portrayed as prominent beneficiaries or agents of the Spirit's work (e.g., Ezek 11:5; Mic 3:8; Isa 48:16; Zech 7:12; see also Hos 9:7; Turner, Spiritual Gifts, 3–4)."[1]

It's not about expanding your own kingdom. It's not about you at all. It's all about Jesus.

The purpose of spiritual gifts is to glorify God by strengthening His people. This is what Paul says in Romans 1:11-12, "For I long to see you, that I may impart to you some spiritual gift to strengthen you – that is, that we may be mutually encouraged by each other's faith, both yours and mine." When Christians serve together in the Spirit everyone is blessed as the people being served are strengthened, and the person serving is blessed to be used of God to benefit others.

There is a great freedom and flexibility in the Spirit regarding how and when various gifts are manifested. Spiritual gifts, "range from the rather ordinary (serving, 1 Pet. 4:11) to the really extraordinary (miracles, 1 Cor. 12:10, 28). In function they range from single events (martyrdom, 1 Cor. 12:10, 28) to ongoing offices (apostles, pastor-teachers, Eph. 4:11). Some gifts appear to represent a special ability recognized only in certain individuals (interpreting, 1 Cor. 14:28); others seem to be a heightened capacity for what is expected of every Christian (showing mercy, Rom. 12:8)."[2]

Sadly, the proper exercise of spiritual gifts has divided some Christians into two groups – cessationists and continuationists – with both groups needing to remember to obey Ephesians 4:3, where Paul commands us to be "eager to maintain the unity of the Spirit."

---

[a] 1 Corinthians 7:7

CHAPTER 2
HAS SPIRIT-FILLED MINISTRY CEASED OR CONTINUED?

As a college freshman at a state university, God saved me largely through just reading the Bible that my girlfriend and now wife Grace gave me. I got plugged in to a healthy, Bible teaching church that was a huge help to establishing my faith in Christ. As I got to know other Christians on campus, they would invite me to their various college ministries and churches, and I quickly realized that different Christians do things differently.

In worship, some groups raised their hands in song while others did not. In some ministries, people were speaking out loud in a language I had never heard that they called "tongues", and I was not sure what happening. In one group, someone took the microphone and said they had a word from God that they wanted to share with the group. I'd never seen anything like these, and numerous other things, in the Catholic Church I stopped attending in my teen years.

I started studying spiritual gifts in the Bible trying to make sense of what was going on in the lives of others around me, and then some supernatural things started to happen in my own life. At my first men's retreat, God spoke to me audibly on a hike telling me to do four things: 1. Marry Grace 2. Preach the Bible 3. Train men 4. Plant churches. I did not know God still spoke to people like this, so I asked my pastor what he thought. He was and is a very godly, humble, wise man of God that I am grateful was my first pastor. He said it was a word from God for me and that was the calling on my life – so I've been doing those very things every day since and God has been supernaturally gracious and generous every step of the journey.

Before long, I also started to have demonic manifestations, sometimes alone and sometimes with Grace also present. Throughout my now 25 years as a senior pastor, preaching and teaching through books of the Bible, I have had prophetic words from God for groups ranging from one person to a stadium filled with people. I have received visions while awake, seeing events that I will explain later in this book. I have also had numerous prophetic dreams while asleep that was like watching a movie of the future that comes to pass exactly as I saw it. I will also explain these events more thoroughly later in this book. I had no background in the supernatural, was not seeking it, and did not, at first, understand it when it happened. So, I spent a lot of time studying the supernatural and consider it a tremendous honor to seek to help your understanding as well. Thank you for that honor.

In hearing about these kinds of experiences, if they trouble you or cause you concern, you are probably more familiar with teaching that is called cessationism. If this all seems rather normal to you and part of your Christian experience, you are probably more familiar with teaching that is called continuationism.

Spiritual gifts are sometimes divided into the categories of sign gifts and service gifts, or the categories of sign gifts, service gifts, and speaking gifts. Within the church, there are two categories of belief with regard to whether all of the spiritual gifts continue to function in the Church today.

Cessationism

Cessationists believe that the sign gifts of the Spirit (for example, miracles, healings, speaking in tongues, private extrabiblical revelation, casting out demons) have ceased. According to cessationism, these sign gifts served a unique role in the first century as a confirmation both of apostolic authority and of the apostolic message prior to the close of the canon of Scripture. Since the Bible is complete, we no longer need sign gifts in order to know what the message of God is. We can simply read the Bible, which has God's completed message. It is important to note that cessationists do not believe that all spiritual gifts have ceased. Cessationism deals only with the sign gifts (e.g prophecy, healing, tongues, demonic deliverance).

A subsection of cessationism includes those who are "open but cautious." This is a growing group of people who believe that sign gifts and the miraculous are possible but highly unlikely today. Consequently, when the presence of such a gift is claimed, it is to be treated with some skepticism. Cessationists typically believe that the sign gifts no longer function as they did during the New Testament era, but that God can, as He desires, theoretically perform similar miracles. They are often theoretical continuationists but practical cessationists. They don't want to limit God by saying God cannot do something supernatural but do so in effect by saying He won't do something supernatural.

Cessationist tribes include most fundamental groups – conservative Baptists, the more conservative wings of the Reformed tribe, and those holding to older forms of dispensational theology. They generally look to Bible teachers such as John MacArthur, Richard Gaffin, Tom Schreiner, B.B. Warfield, J. Gresham Machen, and Daniel B. Wallace.

Continuationism

Continuationists believe that the sign gifts of the Spirit continue and have not ceased as the Spirit still works through gifts such as prophecy, knowledge, tongues, and healings in various ways. Sometimes continuationism is also referred to as being charismatic or Pentecostal.

Continuationists teach about and practice the supernatural gifts in a wide variety of ways. Conservative continuationists prefer order in their gathered church services and place Scripture and godly church leaders in the position to discern what is from the Holy Spirit and what is not. Others are much more open when it comes to claims of prophecies, promises, and healings so that their worship gatherings have less order and leadership in favor of individual freedom of expression with numerous people speaking in tongues without interpretation, giving personal words or prophecies, and other public actions. Continuationist tribes include Charismatics and Pentecostals, denominations like the Assemblies of God, movements like the Jesus Movement that included the Vineyard and Calvary Chapel, and Bible teachers like Jack Hayford, Gordon Fee, Wayne Grudem, R.T. Kendall, and Chuck Smith.

Cessationism often points to such thing as spiritual excesses, unfulfilled prophecies, abuses of spiritual authority, and preference for new revelation over Scripture to call into question and suspicion whether or not much of what is said to be of the Spirit is actually of the flesh or demonic. Paul rebukes the church in Corinth for this, and we will examine shortly. Their warnings are sometimes worthy of consideration as Jesus said in Matthew 12:39, "An evil and adulterous generation seeks for a sign, but no sign will be given to it except the sign of the prophet Jonah." Jesus' point is that some people get so focused on the gifts of God that they lose sight of God, and for that they will face judgment.

Continuationism often points the immutability of God and that He does not change, which would logically mean He does not change the way He works.[a] Furthermore, the Bible does warn us, "do not grieve the Holy Spirit"[b], "Do not quench the Spirit"[c], and that "...stiff-necked people...always resist the Holy Spirit".[d] Admittedly, it is possible to miss out on the fullness of what God has for us if we are not fully submitted and surrendered to the Spirit.

Cessationism sees the abuses of spiritual gifts and, in an effort to prevent

---

[a] Malachi 3:6; Hebrews 13:8 [b] Ephesians 4:30 [c] 1 Thessalonians 5:19 [d] Acts 7:51

error, sometimes overreact by negating the spiritual gift altogether. The abuse of a gift should not negate the use of a gift. For example, perhaps the most abused spiritual gift is teaching as the world is filled with bad instruction that is more comical than Biblical. However, the abuse of teaching should not cause us to abandon teaching the Bible but rather encourage us to teach sound doctrine and warn people about false teachers. I have pretty much always been a continuationist since the Lord saved me at age 19 in college. The first church I was on staff at was cessationist, and the seminary I graduated from leaned in that direction when I was a student. Many, if not most, of the theological councils I have served on were largely, if not mainly, cessationist. Today, most of my ministry friends and partners are continuationist. I wish that there were more conversations between these groups rather than about one another. Knowing many of the leaders in both groups, they both have concerns about excesses done in the name of the Spirit as they both are fully committed to the Scriptures as the perfect Word of God.

Blasphemy of the Holy Spirit

One thing that all Christians (continuationists and cessationists) should be concerned about in relation to spiritual gifts is blasphemy of the Holy Spirit. "'Blasphemy against the Holy Spirit' occurs only in the Synoptic Gospels.[a] In the Matthew and Mark accounts, religious leaders (Pharisees, scribes) offer an alternative explanation for Jesus' powers of exorcism – He is a magician and exercises power by Beelzebul, the prince of demons (i.e., Satan). In this context, Jesus teaches that anyone who verbally attributes the works of the Spirit to Satan commits blasphemy against the Holy Spirit."[3]

There are two ways to blaspheme the Holy Spirit.

One, when God does something, you can negate it by saying it is demonic. As a new pastor, I had some students in our college ministry who loved the Lord and had a private prayer language in tongues. As a new Christian wanting to learn about this experience I had not personally had, I asked a pastor I respected what he thought about it. He told me that other religions had similar ecstatic utterances and so it was probably evidence of a demonic spirit. I loved this pastor, but he may have been guilty of blaspheming the Holy Spirit.

Two, when the demonic does something, you can deceive by saying it is of God. What God creates, Satan counterfeits. God creates: "In the beginning, God created..."[b] Satan counterfeits what God creates: "the work of Satan...counterfeit

---

[a] Matt 12:31; Mark 3:28–29; Luke 12:10 [b] Genesis 1:1

power and signs and miracles. He will use every kind of evil deception..."[a] My wife's father, Gib, faithfully pastored a small church for more than four decades before he passed away. Near his church was a large spiritual organization that said it was a church but had some very bizarre teachings and practices. Grandpa Gib, as our kids called him, was a very gracious and kind man who met with the leader of this cult many times seeking to help correct his error in love. As I began to do ministry in the area, my wife Grace and I attended a service to see for ourselves. The pastor did not mention the Bible and spoke for hours about his personal visions and private revelations from God. He taught on his doctrine of "soul connecting" where God permitted married couples to also connect with someone other than their spouse as their soul mate. As the band starting to play, people began romantically dancing with someone other than their spouse. This adultery of the heart would lead to adultery of the hands as the entire church was caught up in serial adultery based upon the visions from a pastor who repeatedly claimed his revelation came from the Holy Spirit, which was blasphemy of the Spirit.

The debate between cessationism and continuationism is complicated, but at the epicenter is how to interpret 1 Corinthians 13:8–12:

Love never ends. As for prophecies, they will pass away; as for tongues, they will cease; as for knowledge, it will pass away. For we know in part and we prophesy in part, but when the perfect comes, the partial will pass away. When I was a child, I spoke like a child, I thought like a child, I reasoned like a child. When I became a man, I gave up childish ways. For now we see in a mirror dimly, but then face to face. Now I know in part; then I shall know fully, even as I have been fully known.

I have always been a continuationist since I became a Christian. I have become more certain of this conclusion having now taught or preached through more than half of the books of the Bible verse-by-verse. Entire books of the Bible that I have preached or taught such as Exodus, Daniel, all four gospels, Acts, 1 Corinthians, and Revelation to me would be seemingly impossible to faithfully expound upon as a cessationist. I have also read a stack of books on most every interpretive option for this section of Scripture and in the end have decided two things.

One, cessationism is correct and there is a day chosen by God when many of the spiritual gifts will cease. Paul says this plainly, using the examples of "prophecies" and "knowledge" that will "pass away", and "tongues" that "will

---

[a] 2 Thessalonians 2:9-10 [NLT]

cease".

Two, continuationsim is correct in that the day chosen by God when some spiritual gifts will "pass away" and "cease" is in the future and not the past. When Paul says that the day chosen by God is "when the perfect comes" there are, most broadly speaking, two interpretive options. Cessationists say that the completion of the canon of Scripture now gives us the perfect and highest authority of God's Word and therefore there is no longer the need for extrabiblical or supernatural revelation. To be sure, the Bible is perfect.[a] However, in the context of 1 Corinthians 13, what is spoken of is the future state of eternal perfection that dawns when the Lord Jesus Christ returns to set up His perfect Kingdom. This perfect future day happens when, upon Jesus Christ's Second Coming, "we see" Him "face to face". In context, the perfect is not the closing of the canon of the perfect Bible, but the coming of Jesus Christ to fulfill all the prophecies of the Bible perfectly.

In the perfect Kingdom we won't need any revelation in the form of prophecy or tongues because, "we shall know fully". We won't need the gift of healing because there will be no sickness or death, we won't need the gift of evangelism because the elect will have been fully found with no more converts to reach, and we won't have to cast demons out of anyone because everyone in the Kingdom will only be filled with the Spirit. Until Jesus returns, all of the spiritual gifts are needed as the continuationists teach, and their abuses need to be avoided as the cessationists warn.

Sola Scriptura vs Solo Scriptura

At the heart of the Protestant Reformation were some core commitments that Bible-believing Christians continue to hold in the closed hand as essential Christian convictions. Referred to as the "solas", which is the Latin word for alone, they speak of salvation by grace alone (*sola gratia*) through faith alone (*sola fide*) in Jesus Christ alone (*sola Christus*) so that God alone is glorified (*soli Deo gloria*) based upon the Bible as our highest authority (*sola Scriptura*). There is a significant difference between "*sola Scriptura*" (Scripture as our highest authority), and "*solo Scriptura*" (Scripture as our only authority).

The foundation of current cessationism was laid by Princeton Theologian B.B. Warfield in his book *Inerrancy*. Generally speaking, he has made some wonderful theological contributions, but on this issue, his effort to defend the Bible actually leads to a misreading of the Bible. In an effort to defend the Bible against other

---

[a] Psalm 19:7, Proverbs 30:5

authorities such as tradition (common in Catholicism), reason (common in more rationalistic worldly Christianity), or supernatural event (common in more Charismatic and Pentecostal circles), he downplayed other forms of revelation to the degree that others have pretty much denied it.

The problem with having the Bible as your only authority is that the Bible, while our highest authority or metaphorical Supreme Court, itself mentions other authorities that serve as lower courts of revelation. For example, the Bible mentions books and thought leaders that are not Christian but are quoted as saying truthful things. In the Old Testament, this includes the Book of the Wars of the Lord[a], the Book of Jasher[b], the Acts of Solomon[c], the Annals of the Kings of Israel[d], the annals of the kings of Judah[e], the records of Samuel[f], the records of Nathan[g], the records of Shemaiah the prophet and Iddo the seer[h], the annals of Jehu[i], the acts of Uzziah[k], and the Laments of Jeremiah[m]. Some New Testament scholars cite over a hundred such occurrences of non-Christians being quoted in the Bible for speaking truth including Epimenides[n], Aratus[o], the book of Enoch[p], and the Epistle to the Laodiceans.[q]

The Bible also mentions angels who are messengers for God that appear in about 90% of the books of the Bible some 300 times, along with other divine beings referred to as the "sons of God" and "the gods". As messengers, they give true revelation. God speaks throughout the Bible through visions to people who are awake and dreams to people who are asleep including Abram[r], Joseph[s], Isaiah[t], Ezekiel[u], Jeremiah[v], Daniel[w], Zechariah[x], Joseph[y], Stephen[z], Paul[aa], and the entire book of Revelation, which is a series of visions given to John.

God sometimes simply speaks audibly throughout the Scriptures. Examples include Adam and Eve[bb], Moses[cc], Saul[dd], all of Israel from Mount Sinai[ee], and the Father speaking over Jesus at His baptism and transfiguration.[ff] God is also known to occasionally get very creative in revelation, including speaking to Moses through a burning bush[gg] and Balaam through a donkey that may have sounded like Eddie Murphy in Shrek.[hh]

To be perfectly clear, I am fully committed to every word of the Bible as the

---

[a] Numbers 21:14-15 [b] Joshua 10:13 [c] 1 Kings 11:41 [d] 1 Kings 14:19 [e] 1 Kings 15:7 [f] 1 Chronicles 29:29 [g] 1 Chronicles 9:29 [h] 2 Chronicles 12:15 [i] 2 Chronicles 20:34 [k] 2 Chronicles 26:22 [m] 2 Chronicles 35:25 [n] Titus 1:12-13 [o] Acts 17:28 [p] Jude 1:4, 6, 13-15; 2 Peter 2:4, 3:13, John 7:38 [q] Colossians 4:16 [r] Genesis 15 [s] Genesis 37:1-11 [t] Isaiah 6 [u] Ezekiel 1:1 [v] Jeremiah 1:11-14 [w] Daniel 7-8 [x] Luke 1:22 [y] Matthew 1:20-21, 2:13 [z] Acts 7:54-56 [aa] 1 Corinthians 12 [bb] Genesis 3:8 [cc] Exodus 3:4-6 [dd] Acts 9:3-7 [ee] Exodus 20:1-22 [ff] Matthew 4:13-17, 17:1-6 [gg] Exodus 3:4-6 [hh] Numbers 22

Word of God. I have spent more than half my life preaching and teaching God's Word starting with a Bible study in my dorm room at college. At the age of 50, I have spent 25 of my now 50 years in the pulpit preaching through books of the Bible as a senior pastor, in addition to years teaching as a college pastor.

The Bible is the highest court of ultimate authority. However, under the Bible are lower courts of additional authority. The Bible makes this plain, and my point is simply that people who want to argue that the Bible is the only way that God speaks are not consistent with what the Bible teaches. To be Biblical, we must not simply say we believe the Bible, but actually believe everything it says and test every other form of possible revelation by what it says. This is particularly true with spiritual gifts, which we will explore next.

In the perfect Kingdom we won't need any revelation in the form of prophecy or tongues because, "we shall know fully".

CHAPTER 3
UNDERSTANDING SPIRITUAL GIFTS

My wife Grace and I have had the joyful honor of being mom and dad to five kids – three boys and two girls. Growing up, the three boys all loved playing baseball, and our oldest daughter was an all-state sprinter in track. The one child that was not much into athletics was our youngest daughter.

One day, she noticed that her siblings all had trophies in their bedrooms that they had won playing sports. Suddenly, her heart sank as she realized that she would never earn a trophy. Looking into her big blue eyes with my hand on her blonde hair, I explained to her that that everyone has gifts, but that she was a gift. To remind her that I loved her not just because of what she did, but who she was, I had a custom trophy made just for her. The "Sunshine Award" is a very large pink trophy that I presented to her because her presence was sunshine in my life, unlike most anyone else I had ever met.

When it comes to spiritual gifts, it is important to remember that God the Holy Spirit does not just give us gifts, but the light of His presence in our lives is the greatest gift. The gifts of the Spirit are additional blessings and benefits to those who are gifted with the Holy Spirit upon salvation.

The Holy Spirit is THE Gift

At Pentecost, when the Spirit of God came in power on Jewish people, we read in Acts 2:38, "Peter said to them, 'Repent and be baptized every one of you in the name of Jesus Christ for the forgiveness of your sins, and you will receive the gift of the Holy Spirit...'" Later, when the gift of the Holy Spirit came in power on Gentile people, we read in Acts 10:45, "the believers from among the circumcised who had come with Peter were amazed, because the gift of the Holy Spirit was poured out even on the Gentiles." The "gift" is the "Holy Spirit" who gives Himself to us at salvation and gives us also gifts to do ministry to others in partnership with Him.

Regarding the Holy Spirit and spiritual gifts, the most extensive explanation is found in 1 Corinthians 12-14. There, new Christians saved from a completely reprobate culture, very much like our current culture, are getting coached and corrected, which everyone needs to rightly understand spiritual gifts.

Getting a Gift vs Using a Gift

1 Corinthians 12:1 – Now concerning spiritual gifts, brothers, I do not want you to be uninformed.

Oftentimes in life, we get a gift but have no idea how to use it. For example, when each of our five children got their driver's permit, we bought them a car, but the last thing we would do is simply hand them the keys in hopes that they figured out how to drive on the freeway. In addition to the gift, they needed teaching and coaching to learn how to best use the gift. This same principle is true of spiritual gifts as the Spirit gives them, and then we learn how to use them. Paul opened his letter telling the Corinthian church "you are not lacking in any gift".[a] Despite being incredibly gifted, the church was both immature and confused, which is why they sent Paul a list of questions, with his stern rebukes and responses comprising 1-2 Corinthians.

Importantly, Paul not only writes his letter, but he intends for it to be read and obeyed in the church by God's people together in community. This simple fact is vital. You cannot rightly understand or apply the Word of God without the Spirit of God in you and the people of God around you. In the same way, every parent knows that you cannot just give a child information and expect them to learn all they need to know and become who God intends for them to be unless they are also surrounded by modeling and correcting from loving parents.

A healthy church operates like a big family.

What is true when we are born is also true when we are born again. The child of God easily misunderstands what is taught and being in relationship with more mature people who act as spiritual mothers and fathers, along with spiritual big brothers and big sisters, help us to learn by not just hearing what is taught but also seeing how it is applied.

God Creates vs Satan Counterfeits

1 Corinthians 12:2-3 – [2]You know that when you were pagans you were led astray to mute idols, however you were led. [3]Therefore I want you to understand that no one speaking in the Spirit of God ever says "Jesus is accursed!" and no one can

---

[a] 1 Corinthians 1:7

say "Jesus is Lord" except in the Holy Spirit.

When someone is new to Christian faith, they bring with them their beliefs and behaviors that are completely opposed to the Kingdom of God. We all start in the culture of the world, which is how people live hell up before they meet God and start to live Heaven down.

The new Christians in Corinth had been raised like most pagans in our own day. Their big city had a lot of gender confusion including transgenderism, sexual sin, drunkenness, dark spirituality parading as enlightenment, complete with a pagan temple employing upwards of a thousand male and female prostitutes, and anything could be considered the opposite of wisdom or self-control. They probably even had rainbow stickers on their camels. To be faithful to Christ, they needed to avoid what missionaries call "syncretism". Syncretism is what happens when people keep their old beliefs and behaviors and try to add Christianity to them. The result is a diluted and polluted spirituality that is not faithful to God. Many religions and spiritualities, including demonic occultic practices, have such things as ecstatic utterances that are the counterfeit of Christian tongues, healings and powerful miracles that are counterfeits of God's power much like also happened in Egypt during the Exodus, and people who have dreams and visions that come from demons to deceive people. The point is simple – what God creates, Satan counterfeits.

Paul teaches this vital truth speaking in 2 Thessalonians 2:9-10 [NLT] of "the work of Satan...[with] counterfeit power and signs and miracles. He will use every kind of evil deception..." The Christian is not to be vaguely spiritual, but very Spirit-filled.

Demonic counterfeits require discernment, and the ability to distinguish what God creates and Satan counterfeits – including the counterfeit of spiritual gifts. At my first job, I worked as a clerk at a convenience store in a poor neighborhood. One of the first things I learned was how to tell the difference between real money created by the government, and counterfeit currency intended to deceive me into accepting it as real. Regarding the real and counterfeit in the spirit-world, 1 John 4:1-6 says, "Beloved, do not believe every spirit, but test the spirits to see whether they are from God, for many false prophets have gone out into the world. By this you know the Spirit of God: every spirit that confesses that Jesus Christ has come in the flesh is from God, and every spirit that does not confess Jesus is not from God. This is the spirit of the antichrist...Little children, you are from God and have overcome them, for he who is in you is greater than he who is in the world. They are from the world...We are from God. Whoever knows God listens to us; whoever is not from God does not listen to us. By this we know the Spirit of truth and the spirit of error."

The entire point of ministry and spiritual gifts according to Paul in Romans and 1 John is to reveal the Lordship of Jesus Christ as supreme over all people and things. Therefore, if someone says they are a Christian or want to do ministry, but they do not affirm the Lordship of Jesus Christ, they do not have the Holy Spirit. The primary evidence of a person having the Holy Spirit is their love and submission to Jesus and the primary evidence of their ministry service is honor and glory to Jesus Christ alone as Lord.

Giver vs Gifts

1 Corinthians 12:4-7 – ⁴Now there are varieties of gifts, but the same Spirit; ⁵and there are varieties of service, but the same Lord; ⁶and there are varieties of activities, but it is the same God who empowers them all in everyone. ⁷To each is given the manifestation of the Spirit for the common good...

The Christian concept of God is unlike any other in all of human history. Some religions teach that there is one god, or monotheism. Some religions teach that there are many gods, or polytheism. The Bible reveals God as a Trinity, which is one God in three persons – Father, Son, and Spirit. God is by nature relational, and to be made in His image and likeness is to be created for a relationship with God and others.

The Holy Spirit, through Paul, teaches that the entire Trinity is involved in giving each believer their spiritual gift(s). This includes the Holy "Spirit" who gives various gifts, the same "Lord" Jesus Christ who rules over all churches and Christians, as well the same "God" our Father who oversees the entire process of our saving in Christ and sending in Christian service.

Physical Body vs Church Body

Unity

1 Corinthians 12:12-13 – ¹²For just as the body is one and has many members, and all the members of the body, though many, are one body, so it is with Christ. ¹³For in one Spirit we were all baptized into one body—Jews or Greeks, slaves or free—and all were made to drink of one Spirit.

The human body is an engineering marvel to behold. The more medicine learns about how intricate all of the precise details of our physical life work together so that we can live in our body, the more astonished we are.

Paul begins by comparing the local church to a human body. Psalm 139:14 says that we are "fearfully and wonderfully made". Amazingly, the human body has some 206 bones, 650 skeletal muscles, and 210 types of cells. The ability of the body to function as one is staggering.

Just like you live your life and accomplish your tasks through your physical body, so too God works through the church body, which is the physical presence of His people on the earth empowered by His spiritual presence of the Holy Spirit. Just as the various parts of our body work together, so the church is to be filled with people who work together for God's kingdom with the unified effort of a healthy body. This unity on Team Jesus is to exist despite race, generation, gender, spiritual gift, ministry passion, culture, income, education, and other differences, because the same Holy Spirit indwells, gifts, and empowers every Christian as the source of their unity. This explains why the Church of Jesus Christ is the largest, most diverse, and longest-lasting movement of any kind in world history – all held together by the same Spirit that unites us as the body of Christ. This unity of Christ's church body is the theme of 1 Corinthians 12, which we will examine in detail.

Diversity
1 Corinthians 12:14-18 – ¹⁴For the body does not consist of one member but of many. ¹⁵If the foot should say, "Because I am not a hand, I do not belong to the body," that would not make it any less a part of the body. ¹⁶And if the ear should say, "Because I am not an eye, I do not belong to the body," that would not make it any less a part of the body. ¹⁷If the whole body were an eye, where would be the sense of hearing? If the whole body were an ear, where would be the sense of smell? ¹⁸But as it is, God arranged the members in the body, each one of them, as he chose.

Despite the unity that exists in the Church by the power of the Holy Spirit, there is still supposed to be a great diversity of people. Unity is not uniformity, but rather diversity that is brought together by the common characteristics of Spirit-enabled love for Jesus, submission to Scripture, commitment to the Church, and mission to bring the truth and love of the Father to people in the culture. In any healthy church, people will disagree on secondary issues and press one another to deeper study of the Word and love for one another. There will be a wide variety of perspectives and contributions based upon how God has designed them along with the life experiences that shape them and a broad assortment of gifts, talents, abilities, perspectives, and skills.

In this way, a healthy church operates like a big family. In any family, each person has their own unique personality, strengths, and weaknesses, and makes their own unique contribution. Just as a healthy family has unity around what matters, and diversity around who we are and how we do things, so too there must be some diversity in God's family the Church.

Interdependence

1 Corinthians 12:19-21 – ¹⁹If all were a single member, where would the body be? ²⁰As it is, there are many parts, yet one body. ²¹The eye cannot say to the hand, "I have no need of you," nor again the head to the feet, "I have no need of you."

When our kids were little, I made the mistake of letting one of them pack themselves for a trip. When we arrived at our destination, I opened their little backpack to find they had packed a lot of toys and shoes, but no clothes. They literally had over a dozen action figures, and no underwear. An unhealthy church is a lot like that backpack – there is not enough appreciation for the interdependence of diversity.

Just as God has arranged our human body with its various parts to work together effectively, so too He has also arranged the church body with diverse people to work together as one. This means that the specializations in the Church should not lead to division but mutual love and respect. Christian should seek to find the place that God intends for them to serve as a vital part of a local church family. Additionally, we should not think that people with our gifts are godly, and people who are not excited about our calling are less spiritual. God calls some people to go to the mission field and others to stay at home and sleep in their bed. God calls some people to sell all they have to the poor and calls others to grow their business. God calls some people to fast and pray and calls other people to throw parties for feasting and celebrating. Paul says that we should not judge godly people for being different than us, and instead let Jesus the judge of us all do that job. Romans 14:4 says, "Who are you to pass judgment on the servant of another? It is before his own master that he stands or falls. And he will be upheld, for the Lord is able to make him stand." We need each other, and we do not need to judge one another.

Worth

1 Corinthians 12:22-26 – ²²On the contrary, the parts of the body that seem to be weaker are indispensable, ²³and on those parts of the body that we think less honorable we bestow the greater honor, and our unpresentable parts *are treated with greater modesty, [24]which our more presentable parts do not require. But God has so composed the body, giving greater honor to the part that lacked it, [25]that there may be no division in the body, but that the members may have the same care for one another. [26]If one member suffers, all suffer together; if one member is honored, all rejoice together.*

Unlike culture where various people are considered more valuable than others because they are beautiful, smart, talented, rich, etc., the economy of the church is altogether different. This means that every Christian is vitally important and contributes something to the church body, as God designed them to. Much like our own body, those parts of the church that are strong can help carry people who are weak. And, like the parts of our body that we need but do not like to show to others, our church includes important people who probably should not get a microphone and stage time any more than you should put a picture of your liver on your Christmas card instead of your face. In the church, every Christian who is willing to function as a part of the body is deemed worthy of love, respect, and participation because they bear God's image, are filled with God's Spirit, and are equally a part of the church family, though they may not be given the same level of public profile. In addition to spiritual gifts, people also have degrees of Christian maturity which should determine a person's level of leadership and influence, as we will study next.

CHAPTER 4
CHRISTIAN MINISTRY AND CHRISTIAN MATURITY

1 Corinthians 13:1-8, 13 – ¹If I speak in the tongues of men and of angels, but have not love, I am a noisy gong or a clanging cymbal. ²And if I have prophetic powers, and understand all mysteries and all knowledge, and if I have all faith, so as to remove mountains, but have not love, I am nothing. ³If I give away all I have, and if I deliver up my body to be burned, but have not love, I gain nothing. ⁴Love is patient and kind; love does not envy or boast; it is not arrogant ⁵or rude. It does not insist on its own way; it is not irritable or resentful; ⁶it does not rejoice at wrongdoing, but rejoices with the truth. ⁷Love bears all things, believes all things, hopes all things, endures all things. ⁸Love never ends...¹³So now faith, hope, and love abide, these three; but the greatest of these is love.

One of the world's most beloved cookies is the Oreo. It is a brilliant combination of two chocolate wafers held together by vanilla frosting. Without the frosting, there we be no such thing as the Oreo, and the world would be a sadder place for this loss.

In 1 Corinthians 12 and 14, Paul talks about the chocolate wafer of spiritual gifts. In 1 Corinthians 13, Paul reminds us of the vanilla frosting of love that holds it all together. Without love, a gifted church or ministry simple falls apart and does not hold together. Therefore, love is not secondary but primary to every ministry and every spiritual gift.

In 1 Corinthians 13, Paul is communicating one large concept, namely that there is a difference between spiritual giftedness and spiritual maturity. Spiritual giftedness is God's enabling of us to serve Him in fruitful ministry. However, spiritual giftedness alone is not sufficient for us to be like Jesus or for our church to be unified and loving as Jesus intends. Therefore, spiritual maturity is at least as important as spiritual giftedness. Spiritual maturity is marked by love. Practically, this means that despite the difference of gifting and ministry, every Christian is to use their gifts in such a way that others know they are loved by God, the church, and the person who is ministering to them. Apart from loving maturity, giftedness is simply an opportunity to do great harm.

For any spiritual gift to be rightly manifested in ministry, it must be accompanied with love as defined by the character of Christ. Read the list above and put the name of Jesus in every time it says "love" and you will see that the definition of love is the silhouette of Jesus Christ. Then, put your name in every time it says "love" and if you are convicted by the Holy Spirit, stop and ask Him to help you manifest more of the fruit of the Spirit, which is love.[a]

Public vs Private Worship

1 Corinthians 14:1-19 – [1]Pursue love, and earnestly desire the spiritual gifts, especially that you may prophesy. [2]For one who speaks in a tongue speaks not to men but to God; for no one understands him, but he utters mysteries in the Spirit. [3]On the other hand, the one who prophesies speaks to people for their upbuilding and encouragement and consolation. [4]The one who speaks in a tongue builds up himself, but the one who prophesies builds up the church. [5]Now I want you all to speak in tongues, but even more to prophesy. The one who prophesies is greater than the one who speaks in tongues, unless someone interprets, so that the church may be built up. [6]Now, brothers, if I come to you speaking in tongues, how will I benefit you unless I bring you some revelation or knowledge or prophecy or teaching? [7]If even lifeless instruments, such as the flute or the harp, do not give distinct notes, how will anyone know what is played? [8]And if the bugle gives an indistinct sound, who will get ready for battle? [9]So with yourselves, if with your tongue you utter speech that is not intelligible, how will anyone know what is said? For you will be speaking into the air. [10]There are doubtless many different languages in the world, and none is without meaning, [11]but if I do not know the meaning of the language, I will be a foreigner to the speaker and the speaker a foreigner to me. [12]So with yourselves, since you are eager for manifestations of the Spirit, strive to excel in building up the church. [13]Therefore, one who speaks in a tongue should pray that he may interpret. [14]For if I pray in a tongue, my spirit prays but my mind is unfruitful. [15]What am I to do? I will pray with my spirit, but I will pray with my mind also; I will sing praise with my spirit, but I will sing with my mind also. [16]Otherwise, if

---

[a] Galatians 5:22

you give thanks with your spirit, how can anyone in the position of an outsider say "Amen" to your thanksgiving when he does not know what you are saying? [17]For you may be giving thanks well enough, but the other person is not being built up. [18]I thank God that I speak in tongues more than all of you. [19]Nevertheless, in church I would rather speak five words with my mind in order to instruct others, than ten thousand words in a tongue.

As a young pastor, for a few years I oversaw an all-ages punk rock concert venue for mainly non-Christian teenagers. We gave young bands a start at live shows to test the viability of their musical ability.

Some bands were incredibly tight – their rhythm section dominated by the drummer and bass player stayed in steady unison driving the guitars and vocals forward like a finely tuned machine. Some bands were they exact opposite. Losing time, forgetting the lyrics, or having different band members playing different songs all at the same time was the acoustic equivalent of a series of head-on collisions among vehicles all converging on an intersection at high speed. In this section, Paul begins by using the analogy of a band speaking of the "flute", "harp", "bugle" and "notes" to distinguish between public and private worship to God.

Your private worship to God is a lot like a new musician first learning an instrument. At home, alone, you make a lot of bad noise until you figure out how to play some good music. Some people forget this basic principle and want to come practice their gift on the stage at the church during service – they want to sing, preach, speak in tongues, or prophesy, but they are not yet ready to go public and everyone in the church should not be forced to watch anyone and everyone turn the church into what feels more like open mic night at a dive bar after a few drinks. There is a big difference between your private and public worship. Your soul may benefit from you singing at the top of your lungs completely out of pitch and key in your car, but you do not need a sound system and church service for that. Your soul may benefit from praying loudly in tongues in the basement of your home as you emotionally process a difficult season with God, but that need not be livestreamed to the world. Your soul may benefit from you praying at the top of your lungs for people you have a burden for, but if everyone did that at church, it would be as edifying as a riot.

Private worship is for you, public worship is for everyone else and not all about you. Private worship is for self-care, but when you make your private worship public, you are being selfish. When the church comes together, it is not time for you to express yourself, or do what you do in private. Instead, the goal is to find harmony with the rest of God's people and, like a band, work together in unison and harmony to love and serve the Lord. To help God's people find the rhythm of public worship together in the Spirit, the following questions are helpful while looking at the passage above from 1 Corinthians 14:

1. What will other people find loving (14:1)?
2. What will build up those who are struggling (14:3)?
3. What will encourage those who are discouraged (14:3)?
4. How can I benefit other people and not just myself (14:4,6)?
5. How can I build the whole church up (14:4-5,12)?
6. What will help others learn about God most easily (14:9)?
7. What will non-Christians think about what I'm saying/doing and will it help or hinder them to hear about Jesus through Bible teaching (14:16-17)?
8. Am I helping people learn the Bible or hindering that from happening (14:19)?

Spiritual Gifts vs Spiritual Maturity

1 Corinthians 14:20-25 – [20]Brothers, do not be children in your thinking. Be infants in evil, but in your thinking be mature. [21]In the Law it is written, "By people of strange tongues and by the lips of foreigners will I speak to this people, and even then they will not listen to me, says the Lord." [22]Thus tongues are a sign not for believers but for unbelievers, while prophecy is a sign not for unbelievers but for believers. [23]If, therefore, the whole church comes together and all speak in tongues, and outsiders or unbelievers enter, will they not say that you are out of your minds? [24]But if all prophesy, and an unbeliever or outsider enters, he is convicted by all, he is called to account by all, [25]the secrets of his heart are disclosed, and so, falling on his face, he will worship God and declare that God is really among you.

When our five children were little, for some years we lived in a house next to a lake where sailboats would dart across the surface of the water by harnessing and channeling the power of the unseen wind. For fun, I often took our kids for walks to see the sailboats.

Jesus told Nicodemus that the Holy Spirit is a powerful, unseen force like the wind. Much like a sailboat, unless we direct it with the rudder of our mind and will, we can have great energy but not ministry.

Some churches have a rudder but not a sail. They have lots of systems, policies, theology, procedures, and order but never harness the wind of the Spirit to leave the dock of church and venture out to reach the world for Christ. If you've ever been in an old, established, religious church with older saints who have retired from life and God, then you know what this looks like.

Some churches have a sail but not a rudder. They are zealous, filled with passion, and have a sense of urgency and hope that is contagious but end up saying and doing crazy things. If you've ever been with a lot of brand-new, young Christians snatched by God from the flames of hell who are on fire for God but have no idea what they are talking about, then you know what this looks like as well. What Paul is arguing for is the rudder of the Scriptures and the sail of the Spirit so that passion is directed, zeal is focused, and enthusiasm results in ministry instead of a mess.

Order vs Disorder

1 Corinthians 14:26-33,40 – [26]What then, brothers? When you come together, each one has a hymn, a lesson, a revelation, a tongue, or an interpretation. Let all things be done for building up. [27]If any speak in a tongue, let there be only two or at most three, and each in turn, and let someone interpret. [28]But if there is no one to interpret, let each of them keep silent in church and speak to himself and to God. [29]Let two or three prophets speak, and let the others weigh what is said. [30]If a revelation is made to another sitting there, let the first be silent. [31]For you can all prophesy one by one, so that all may learn and all be encouraged, [32]and the spirits of prophets are subject to prophets. [33]For God is not a God of confusion but of peace....[40]But all things should be done decently and in order.

Imagine a city without laws, law enforcement, and justice where everyone did what was right in their own eyes like the days of the Judges and the movie The Purge. Imagine a sports team with no coach or playbook where every player just played whatever position they wanted and ran whatever play they preferred minus any sort of referee to keep the peace.

For any spiritual gift to be rightly manifested in ministry, it must be accompanied with love as defined by the character of Christ.

Imagine a family where there were children but no parents, no rules, no structure, and no authority. Imagine a company where there were numerous employees but no managers or bosses, no job descriptions, no meetings, and no deadlines or performance reviews. Imagine a church where there was no leadership, no expectations, no structures, and everyone did what they thought was best regardless of what anyone else thought. If you want to waste time, energy, and money, create division instead of unity, and discourage and exhaust people on the way to complete meltdown, these are some good examples of how our culture has tried and failed to operate with lawfulness, which only brings awfulness.

Obviously, if our King and His Kingdom are one of honor, order, and decency, then anarchy cannot be our pattern for ministry. As a general rule, spiritual gifts like leadership and administration should help to cause public worship meetings for God's people to resemble the rule and reign of the Prince of Peace and not the Devil of Disorder. However, at times, the Holy Spirit will show up in a surprising way to do some unexpected ministry that is planned by God but seems extemporaneous to us.

In the Bible, Luke uses words like "suddenly" to remind us that God is free and can choose to show up in power unannounced:

·Luke 2:13 – And suddenly there was with the angel a multitude of the heavenly host praising God.

·Luke 21:34 – "But watch yourselves lest your hearts be weighed down with dissipation and drunkenness and cares of this life, and that day come upon you suddenly like a trap."

·Acts 2:2 – And suddenly there came from heaven a sound like a mighty rushing wind, and it filled the entire house where they were sitting.

·Acts 9:3 – Now as he [Saul/Paul] went on his way, he approached Damascus, and suddenly a light from heaven shone around him.

·Acts 16:26 – ...suddenly there was a great earthquake, so that the foundations of the prison were shaken. And immediately all the doors were opened, and everyone's bonds were unfastened.

·Acts 22:6 – "As I [Saul/Paul] was on my way and drew near to Damascus, about noon a great light from heaven suddenly shone around me..."

In moments where God moves suddenly and in unusual power, leaders that are Spirit-filled and Spirit-led need to discern what the will of God is in that moment. Often, those people who are immature – self-confident, pushy, religious, or emotional – will seek to assume leadership in the moment. It is vital for mature leaders filled with the Spirit to discern the will of God in these heightened moments of spiritual breakthrough. Otherwise, the flesh will turn it into a mess, or the demonic will twist it into a mayhem. To help your church or ministry be as healthy and godly as possible, every Christian discovering their spiritual gift(s) and finding their place to serve on Team Jesus is vital. Next, we will look at the serving gifts before we continue by studying the speaking and supernatural gifts in the following chapters.

CHAPTER 5
DISCOVERING YOUR SPIRITUAL GIFT: PART 1 (SERVING GIFTS)

When you are a child, one of the most fascinating things to learn is how base colors are mixed to form a hue of other colors. For example, if you take three primary colors – red, yellow, and blue – you can mix them to make millions of colors with different colors and combinations.

Spiritual gifts are a bit like base colors. God the Holy Spirit gives each Christian believer at least one (and usually numerous) spiritual gifts. We are each also given different portions of a gift, along with a different combination of gifts that combine to give us our unique proverbial color for Christian service.

The goal of this study is to help you find how God has uniquely made you to glorify Him by serving others in ministry. To find your place on Team Jesus a few questions are helpful to get started:

1. What things do you find joy in the Spirit doing?
2. What things have people said you are innately good at?
3. When people ask you for help, is there a common reason they are inviting your help?
4. What people or things do you have a burden for and care about?
5. What people or things do you see that need attention that other people tend to overlook?
6. What abilities has God given you (e.g. athletic ability, sharp mind, natural rhythm or perfect pitch)?
7. What resources has God given you that could be part of your ministry (e.g. wealth to give, a company that you own, technical training, job experience, etc.)?
8. What life experiences has God used to shape your character that could be helpful in ministering to others going through similar things (e.g. an injury or illness, marriage or divorce, parenting or loss of a child, deliverance from an addiction, etc.)?

9. What things energize and motivate you that might deplete or overwhelm someone else?

10. What other things have you learned about God's divine design of you through other resources (e.g. personality tests, vocational assessment tests, etc.)?

Not every Christian is called to vocational ministry, but every Christian is called to the "work of ministry".[a] This ministry work includes your job, your family, church, and community, and loving and serving people in your life on behalf of Jesus Christ.

Spiritual gifts are given by the Holy Spirit to Christians and every Christian has at least one spiritual gift, and some people may have many.[b] Christians are given their spiritual gift solely by God's grace and can do nothing to earn or get a different gift because God chooses our gifts.[c] As Christians, we do not choose our spiritual gifts, as God chooses them for us. Hebrews 2:4 says, "God also bore witness by signs and wonders and various miracles and by gifts of the Holy Spirit distributed according to his will." As Christians, we can all be immature at times. When we are, we covet the gifts of others rather than being content with the gifts we have. Like kids at Christmas, we are supposed to be grateful for the gifts we get to open, and also glad for the other kids who open their boxes to find different gifts than we did. Our Heavenly Father is perfect, and the gifts He chooses for us are best for us and faith is believing this fact and serving as He made us, not as we wished He'd made us.

Perhaps an illustration will help. Many years ago, a very kind young woman was determined to sing in the worship team for a ministry my wife Grace and I were a part of. Her entire family had been very musical for generations, with most everyone able to play multiple instruments and sing. Their informal family times together at home were the equivalent of incredible live concerts. Growing up in this family, she assumed that she was like everyone else and musically gifted. So, we gave her a microphone and what happened next was, to put it nicely, not great. She could not keep the beat or hit the note and struggled mightily. A bit embarrassed, she went home to practice for months, determined to lead worship. Some months later, she tried again...and had made no progress. I felt compassion for her

---

[a] Ephesians 4:12 [b] 1 Corinthians 12:11,18; Hebrews 2:4; 1 Peter 4:10 [c] Romans 12:6; 1 Corinthians 12:4-7,11

as the Bible says to make a joyful noise unto the Lord, and she and I both are good at making noise that is not joyful for others to hear when singing to the Lord. As I talked with her, she felt like she was a failure and had no purpose to her life as she was not able to serve the Lord as she had wanted. In our conversation, she revealed that she was excelling at her job managing employees, balancing finances, and organizing schedules. God had hard-wired her to organize, administrate, and lead. Once she accepted her divine design, she started using her gifts and experiences to organize and lead the entire ministry. She was an incredibly helpful person and, before long, everyone was very grateful for her unique contribution and she found a lot of joy accepting who God made her to be and doing what God made her to do. The more she used her gifts, the more effective and fruitful she became. I want this same sort of experience for you. To help you find your divine design, here are some possible helps:

1. What do Christian friends, and mature Christian leaders who have wisdom, say about how God has gifted you?
2. Have you started by just finding a place to start serving to get started in seeing where God might have a unique fit for you?
3. If you have been serving in an area that is not a great fit, where can you pivot to start serving instead?

As we have established, there are gifts, talents, and abilities that God gives us for ministry that are not listed in the Bible. However, as a general rule those spiritual gifts listed in the Bible fall into three broad categories:

1. Serving gifts – deeds that build the Kingdom of God
2. Speaking gifts – words that build the Kingdom of God
3. Sign gifts – supernatural acts that point to the Kingdom of God

In the remainder of this chapter, we will examine the serving gifts, and then study the speaking and sign gifts in the following two chapters.

Mercy

Place in Scripture: Romans 12:8

Defined: The gift of mercy is the capacity to feel and express unusual compassion, empathy, and sympathy for those in difficult or crisis situations and provide them with the necessary help and support to see them through tough times. People with the gift of mercy and people who are hurting, struggling, broken and overwhelmed find one another so that loneliness can be reduced, a hurt can be healed, and a person at the end of their rope gets a knot to hang on to.

Warning: People with the gift of mercy need to be careful that they do not rush to conclusions by only hearing one side of the story from a hurting person. To accurately assess a pain or problem, both sides must be heard, otherwise the gift of mercy can result in taking up an offense for someone, which only makes matters worse. Proverbs 18:17 says, "The one who states his case first seems right, until the other comes and examines him." Additionally, those with the gift of mercy tend to be less judgmental than others, but they can overlook the ways that a hurting person may be reaping what they have sowed through bad choices in life. To truly be merciful to someone, we need to have compassion for their hardship they are enduring to help them heal up in the present, and also help them see how wiser life choices in the future could greatly help them move forward and avoid repeating the pain in the future.

General makeup: The ability to "walk in another's shoes" and to feel the pain and burdens they carry. They desire to make a difference in the lives of hurting people without being judgmental. People with this gift understand the ministry of presence – that some painful things are hard to explain or fix, but it is a great blessing to have someone sit with you so that you are not alone but comforted.

Seen in Jesus' ministry: Jesus taught on mercy.[a] He is repeatedly described as having compassion which is the most frequent emotion mentioned of Jesus in the Bible[b], and was so filled with mercy that He sometimes wept.[c] Jesus' mercy included an attentiveness to and concern for women including the rejected Samaritan woman[d], the woman caught in adultery[e], a widow[f], a woman with a bleeding disorder[g], and a woman bent over for eighteen years.[h] In the ancient world, single men who were religious leaders did not have much interest in children, but children came to Jesus because He loved them.[i] Jesus' ministry to individual children include Him traveling to the bedside of Jairus' daughter to lovingly heal her, the favorite Bible story of one of our daughters when she was little.[k]

Illustrated biblically: Dorcas "was always doing good and helping the poor".[m] Also, the good Samaritan is one of the most classic stories ever told on the subject of mercy.[n]

---

[a] Matt. 5:7; 9:13; 23:23 [b] Matt. 9:36; 15:32; 23:37; Luke 7:13 [c] John 11:35 [d] John 4:7-26 [e] John 8:10-11 [f] Luke 7:12-13 [g] Luke 8:48 cf. Matthew 9:22; Mark 5:34 [h] Luke 13:12 [i] Matt. 19:14 [k] Luke 8:40-56 [m] Acts 9:36 [n] Luke 10:30–37

Illustrated historically: Amy Carmichael was a missionary of the Dohnavur Fellowship with a compassionate heart for those in need. In India, she witnessed many "child widows", young girls who grew up to be temple prostitutes. In the 20th century, Amy fought this practice by rescuing many girls out of this situation and into the Christian community. She elevated the status of women, showing them that Jesus loved and had compassion for them as the God of all mercy.

Do you have this gift?

1. Do you find yourself being drawn to people who are needy, hurting, sick, overwhelmed, disabled, or elderly?
2. Do you often think of ways to minister to those who are suffering and see people who are hurting but often overlooked?
3. Do you sense a great deal of compassion for people having personal, spiritual, relational, and emotional problems?
4. Do a lot of people choose you as their wise counsel or confidant to talk about issues in their life with you?
5. Are you more of a "feeler" than other people you know who are more of a "thinker"?
6. Do you find that when you visit those who are suffering it brings you joy to share with them rather than it depressing you?
7. Do you find yourself responding to people more out of compassion for what they are going through rather than judgment for the choices they made that contributed to their troubles?
8. Do you tend to see Jesus more as a priest who intercedes for people in love with patient compassion?
9. If you had to define yourself as more tough like Jesus the Lion or tender like Jesus the Lamb, would you pick the tender lamb?

Hospitality

Place in Scripture: Romans 12:13

Defined: Hospitality is the ability to welcome strangers and entertain guests, often in your home, with great joy and kindness so that they become friends. Hospitality is supposed to include one's family[a], friends[b], Christians[c], and strangers who may not be Christians.[d]

---

[a] 1 Tim. 5:8 [b] Prov. 27:10 [c] Gal. 6:10 [d] Lev. 19:34

General makeup: These people tend to have an "open home" where others are welcome to visit. This gift is often combined with abilities like interior design, cooking, and event planning. People with this gift like to find new people, introduce people to each other, host events, throw parties, and create memorable occasions where people can make relationships and memories, which is a way of practicing for the Kingdom.

Warning: Importantly, hospitality is NOT to be extended to evil people or false teachers who Satan sends to harm your family and/or church family.[a] When sheep welcome wolves into the pen, the result is not ministry but misery. For this reason, hospitality also requires discernment.

Seen in Jesus' ministry: Jesus spent time befriending social outcasts[b], often ate with His disciples, and has welcomed us into the family of God, which includes an eternal home[c] and an eternal party.[d] Jesus was very close with two sisters and one brother named Mary, Martha, and Lazarus. He often stayed with them, ate at their home, and their hospitality to Him resulted in a close relationship with them.[e]

Illustrated biblically: Church leaders are to exercise hospitality.[f] Peter enjoyed the hospitality of Simon[g] and Cornelius.[h] Paul enjoyed the hospitality of Lydia[i] and the Philippian jailer.[k] Much like many current churches that have large meetings in public spaces, and small groups in private homes, the early church met in larger areas like the local synagogues and central "temple" as well as, breaking bread in their homes..."[m]

Illustrated historically: In the turbulent social chaos of the 1960's and 70's, God raised up a loving couple to address a lost and rebellious generation with the truth of Jesus Christ. Francis Shaeffer was a widely known apologist, theologian and evangelist. What is not as widely known, though, is the impact his wife had on his ministry. As their renowned pupil Os Guiness said, "Mrs. Schaeffer is the secret of Schaeffer." Together, they built an international ministry in the Swiss Alps called L'Abri, which means shelter. With modest beginnings, their ministry grew quickly as lost university students, eastern mystics, rebellious church kids, hippies and adherents to other faiths from around the world came to visit L'Abri. Francis would teach, debate and give answers for the faith. Edith illustrated it with a life of

---

[a] 2 John 10-11 [b] Matt. 11:19 [c] John 14:2 [d] Isa. 25:6–9; Rev. 19:6–9 [e] Luke 10:38-41; John 12:1-2 [f] 1 Tim. 3:2; Titus 1:8 [g] Acts 9:43 [h] Acts 10:48 [i] Acts 16:15 [k] Acts 16:34 [m] Acts 2:46 cf. Acts 5:42

hospitable service. Over a hundred students would live with them at a time. Edith provided clean bedding, home cooked meals, fresh flowers, neat decor, paintings, sculptures, sketchings, music, endless hot cookies and table settings she considered art. She even published a book titled "The Hidden Art of Homemaking" to teach others about hospitality.

Do you have this gift?

1. Do you enjoy having people in your home?
2. Do you enjoy watching people meet and have fun at parties and events you helped to plan and host?
3. Is your home the kind that most people feel comfortable in and can drop by to visit unannounced?
4. Do you feel that something is really missing in your life when you cannot have guests into your home, host events, throw parties, plan vacations, and have fun on the calendar?
5. When you think of your home, do you view it from the perspective of guests who will visit so that they feel most welcome and relaxed?
6. Do you consider your home as a place of ministry for others and not just a retreat for you?
7. Do you tend to enjoy going all out for birthdays, holidays, and other celebrations?
8. When there is a room full of people having a good time, do you find your joy in seeing their joy?

Discernment

Place in Scripture: 1 Corinthians 12:10

Defined: The spiritual gift of discernment is the ability to quickly perceive whether such things as people, events, or beliefs are from God or Satan.

General makeup: People with the gift of discernment from the Holy Spirit know that Satan and his demons disguise themselves as holy.[a] They also know that Satan empowers counterfeit miracles[b] to deceive people[c], and that he empowers false teachers[d], false prophets[e], false apostles[f], and false doctrines.[g] People with this gift can distinguish more easily and accurately the difference between what God cre-

---

[a] 1 Corinthians 11:14–15 [b] Exodus 7:11–22; 8:7; Matthew 7:21–23; 2 Timothy 3:8 [c] 2 Thessalonians 2:9 [d] 2 Peter 2:1 [e] Matthew 7:15 [f] 2 Corinthians 11:13 [g] 1 Timothy 1:3; 6:3

ates and Satan counterfeits.

<u>Warning:</u> Those with the gift of discernment are more prone to be the first to see a problem with a person, teaching, or ministry. If not careful, they can become negative, jaded, distrusting and critical of others in a way that is unholy and unhelpful. People with the gift of discernment need to operate in faith, hope, and love while seeking to help make things better rather than just pointing out what was wrong.

<u>Seen in Jesus' ministry:</u> Isaiah 11:2 promised that "...the Spirit of the Lord shall rest upon him [Jesus], the Spirit of wisdom and understanding, the Spirit of counsel and might, the Spirit of knowledge and the fear of the Lord." John 2:24-25 [NLT] says, "Jesus didn't trust them, because he knew all about people. No one needed to tell him about human nature, for he knew what was in each person's heart." Jesus was able to know the presence of Satan[a], see when someone was influenced by Satan[b], and know when someone's words were influenced by Satan.[c]

<u>Illustrated biblically:</u> John[d], Paul[e], Peter[f], and the disciples[g] all demonstrated the gift of discernment. In Philippians 1:9-10, Paul said, "it is my prayer that your love may abound more and more, with knowledge and all discernment, so that you may approve what is excellent, and so be pure and blameless for the day of Christ", which is the purpose of discernment.

<u>Illustrated historically:</u> At the beginning of the Protestant Reformation, Martin Luther had a clear belief in the cosmic battle between God and angels and Satan and demons, including speaking against the demonic in the hymn he penned "A Mighty Fortress is our God". A noted historian on Luther wrote an entire book on Luther's experience with and teaching about the devil and his experience with the demonic titled *Luther: Man between God and the Devil*. In his magazine *Table Talk*, Luther wrote of the devil more times than the Bible, gospel, grace, and prayer. Luther also speaks of multiple visits from the devil including appearing in his room at the Castle of Wartburg, Germany, as Luther sat down to translate the Bible. Startled, Luther grabbed his inkwell and threw it at the devil. Luther's discernment brought him to question and correct some erroneous teaching in the Catholic church such as indulgences, purgatory, praying to dead saints, and justification by faith alone without the contribution of any religious works, which he called the issue on which the church stands or falls.

---

[a] Matthew 4:1–11 [b] Luke 22:31 [c] Matthew 16:23 [d] 1 John 4:1 [e] Acts 16:16–18 [f] Acts 5:1–11 [g] Matthew 10:1

Do you have this gift?

1. Have you felt a special responsibility to protect the truth of God's Word by exposing that which is wrong?
2. Do you often make a swift evaluation of someone or something that was said that others did not see, but yet proved to be correct?
3. Do you have a solid understanding of Scripture and a sensitivity to the leading of God the Holy Spirit?
4. Are you keenly aware of moral sin and doctrinal heresy?
5. Can you read a book or hear a teacher and almost immediately uncover any false teaching?
6. Do you have an awareness of demonic presence and how to help people be free of demonic oppression?
7. Do you have a gut feeling about people or things that proves to be right most of the time?
8. Do people who are confused about a doctrine, leader, or teacher often ask you what your evaluation is to help them get clarity amidst confusion?

Helps/Service

Place in Scripture: Romans 12:7; 1 Corinthians 12:28

Defined: The gift of helps/service is the ability to joyfully work alongside others and help them complete the task God has given them. People with this gift generally prefer to work behind the scenes. They also tend to find joy in helping alleviate the burdens and responsibilities of others. This gift is usually accompanied with an attitude of humility and sacrifice, as well as an ability to perceive the needs of others.

General makeup: These people tend to demonstrate a servant attitude, loyalty, attention to detail, and responsiveness to the initiatives of others. They function well in positions of detail and assistant leadership. People with this gift often ask, "what do you need me to do", or "how can I help" and enjoy doing whatever is needed.

Warning: Sometimes, irresponsible people will find people with this gift and dump their duties on them. We need to help people but should not become co-dependent, be unable to say "no", or have people make us do things for them that God wants them to do for themselves.

Seen in Jesus' ministry: Matthew 20:28 says that "the Son of Man [Jesus] did not come to be served, but to serve, and to give his life as a ransom for many." Philippians 2:5–7 says, "Have this mind among yourselves, which is yours in Christ Jesus, who, though he was in the form of God, did not count equality with God a thing to be grasped, but emptied himself, by taking the form of a servant..." Jesus also said, "I am among you as one who serves," and He even washed His disciples' feet which was the job of the lowest servant in a household.[a]

Illustrated biblically: Because servants often work behind the scenes, their work, but not their name, is often mentioned in Scripture.[b] People named in the Bible who helped the church through service include Phoebe, Priscilla, Aquila, Tryphena, Tryphosa[c], and John Mark.[d] The word sometimes translated "deacon" simply means servant and refers to church leaders who have the gift of helps/service.[e]

Illustrated historically: Charles Spurgeon is one of the most well-known preachers of the Christian Church in London during the Victorian era. His wife Susannah was a lovely woman he affectionately called "Susie". As Charles' popularity was skyrocketing, thousands packed into the Surrey Garden's Music Hall to hear him preach. Tragically, some troublemaking critics shouted "fire" which caused a panicked stampede that left may injured and some dead. This event sent Charles into a deep depression that returned in seasons throughout his life. Susie was a constant help to him during his bouts with depression, praying for him, serving him, and doing whatever was best to help him through tough times. Susie was struck with health problems that left her largely bedridden at home for the last half of their marriage. To continue to come alongside her husband, she had her bedroom and his study adjoined so she could be there to talk with and pray for him throughout the day. She also sent him affectionate letters when he was away to encourage and help him carry his large ministry load of responsibility. In starting and leading "Mrs. Spurgeon's Book Fund" she gave away roughly 200,000 books to poor pastors to help them preach God's Word. She is an amazing woman that my wife Grace has enjoyed studying the life and legacy of, and her life was given to helping and serving her husband and sons in their ministry, along with ministers from around the world, even though she was sickly and confined to a bed. Grace gifted me the four-volume C.H. Spurgeon Autobiography, which Susie completed, and it's the most treasured books outside of the Bible in my personal library. What she shares in these books continues to help and serve us to this day.

---

[a] Luke 22:27; John 13:5 [b] e.g., Numbers 11:17; 1 Timothy 6:2; Acts 6:1–3 [c] Romans 16:1–4,12 [d] Acts 13:5 [e] 1 Timothy 3:8–13

Do you have this gift?

1. Do you enjoy helping others become more effective in their work?
2. Do you prefer to labor behind the scenes?
3. When someone is doing a job poorly, is your first instinct to help them succeed instead of criticizing their failure?
4. Do you prefer to work in a supportive role rather than a leadership capacity?
5. When you hear of someone with needs, do you offer your services if possible?
6. When someone asks for your help, do you have difficulty saying no?
7. Do you not necessarily care what your role is as long as you are on a healthy team that is doing good ministry?
8. Do more lowly tasks that other people tend to delegate or avoid not bother you and so you do them?
9. Do you get asked to do a lot of things, join a lot of ministries, and help a lot of people?

Administration

Place in Scripture: 1 Corinthians 12:28

Defined: Administration is the God-given ability to give direction and make decisions on behalf of others that result in efficient operation and accomplishment of goals. Administration includes the ability to organize people, things, information, finances, etc. Often the mark of an administrator is the ability to accomplish things in a "fitting and orderly way".[a]

General makeup: Administrators often have a keen eye for detail. They may also possess the natural talents of organization, observing and using details, problem solving, and reasoning.

Warning: If someone with the gift of administration does not trust leadership, they can become very controlling and try to become the de facto leader through making and enforcing policy, controlling finances, demanding information, and creating cumbersome processes that provide them power. Additionally, people with this gift can lose sight of the big picture and mission as they get overly focused on the small details.

Seen in Jesus' ministry: Jesus organized His ministry by choosing his inner circle of

---

[a] 1 Corinthians 14:40

three disciples[a], appointing the 12[b], and sending out the 72 two-by-two.[c]

Illustrated biblically: Joseph[d], Jethro[e], and Titus[f] all demonstrate the gift of administration. The entire book of Nehemiah is a case study in leadership from an incredibly gifted governmental leader with the gift of administration who rebuilt the city
of Jerusalem after years of neglect.

Illustrated historically: The Irish people were a brutal and pagan people that
Christian missionaries could not successfully find a way to reach until a man that is
now known as Saint Patrick. Saint Patrick is technically not a saint, as he was never
canonized by the Roman Catholic Church. Additionally, Patrick was not actually
Irish. Rather, he was an Englishman and a Roman citizen, who spoke Latin and
a bit of Welsh. Patrick was born around 390 AD. When he was roughly 16 years of
age, he was captured by pirates and taken on a ship to Ireland, where he was sold
into slavery. He spent the next six years alone in the wilderness as a shepherd for
his master's cattle and sheep. Patrick was a rebellious non-Christian teenager who
had come from a Christian family. His grandfather was a pastor, and his father was
a church leader. However, during his extended periods of isolation without any human contact, Patrick began praying and was eventually born again into a vibrant
relationship with Jesus Christ. Patrick endured the years of isolation in rain and
snow by praying up to 100 prayers each day and another 100 each night. In his early
twenties, God spoke to Patrick in a dream, telling him to flee from his master for a
ship that was waiting for him. Amazingly, Patrick made the 200-mile walk without
being caught or harmed and found a ship setting sail for his home, just as God had
promised. The sailors were out of food for the journey, so Patrick prayed. Miracu-
lously, a herd of pigs ran toward the ship, providing a bountiful feast for the long
voyage home. Upon returning home, Patrick enrolled in seminary and was eventually commissioned as a pastor. Some years later, God spoke to Patrick in a dream,
commanding him to return to Ireland to preach the Gospel and plant churches for
the pagans who lived there. The Roman Catholic Church had given up on con-
verting such "barbarians," who were deemed beyond hope. The Celtic peoples, of
which the Irish were part, were an illiterate bunch of drunken, fighting, perverted
pagans. They were such a violent and lawless people, numbering anywhere from
200,000 to 500,000, that they had no city centers or national government and were
spread out among some 150 warring clans. Their enemies were terrified of them

---

[a] Mark 9:2 [b] Mark 3:13–14 [c] Luke 10:1 [d] Genesis 41:41–57; 47:13–26 [e] Exodus 18 [f] Titus 1:5

because they were known to show up for battles and partake in wild orgies before running into battle naked and drunk, screaming as if they were demon-possessed. In faith, the 40-year-old Patrick sold all of possessions, including the land he had inherited from his father, to fund his missionary journey to Ireland. He worked as an itinerant preacher and paid large sums of money to various tribal chiefs to ensure he could travel safely through their lands and preach the Gospel. His strategy was completely unique. He functioned like a missionary, trying to relate to the Irish people and communicate the Gospel in their culture by using such things as three-leaf clovers to explain the Gospel. Upon entering a pagan clan, Patrick would seek to first convert the tribal leaders and other people of influence. He would then pray for the sick, cast demons out of the possessed, preach the Bible, and use both musical and visual arts to persuade people to put their faith in Jesus. If enough converts were present, he would build a simple church that did not resemble ornate Roman architecture, baptize the converts, and hand over the church to a convert he had trained to be the pastor. Then he would move on to repeat the process with another clan. Patrick gave his life to the people who had enslaved him until he died at 77 years of age. He had seen untold thousands of people convert, as between 30-40 of the 150 tribes had become substantially Christian. He trained 1000 pastors, planted 700 churches, and was the first noted person in history to take a strong public stand against slavery.

<u>Do you have this gift?</u>

1. When things are poorly organized do you get frustrated and want to help fix things?
2. Do you like to see resources best stewarded so that things like money, facilities, time, and energy are utilized for the best return on investment?
3. Do you tend to have a risk radar that looks at the downside if things are not done well and seek to safeguard people and organizations by keeping them "buttoned up"?
4. Are you attracted to opportunities where someone needs to bring order out of chaos?
5. Do you naturally organize your life, schedule, finances, priorities, etc.?
6. Do you become energized working on tasks and projects whereas that level of detail work overwhelms or exhausts other people you know?
7. Do things like efficiency and promptness matter more to you than most people you know?

8. Do things like spreadsheets, budgets, organizational charts and software, files, and highlighters make you happy?

9. Do you tend to see Jesus more as a King who rules a perfectly architected and led Kingdom?

Giving

Place in Scripture: Romans 12:8

Defined: Giving is the ability to give money and other forms of wealth joyfully, wisely, and generously to meet the needs of others and help support ministries.

General makeup: Regardless of the amount, people with this gift genuinely view their treasures, talents, and time as on loan from God and not their own. They are often moved to meet the physical needs of others. They enjoy giving of themselves and what they have. Even if they do not possess the resources to help, they earnestly pray for those needs to be met.

Warning: Some people who are greedy or manipulative take advantage of people with this gift by seeking to benefit themselves in an ungodly way. Learning to say "no" to everything so you can say "yes" to the things God has for you to give to is critical so that you are not just generous, but also a good steward.

Seen in Jesus' ministry: Roughly 25% of Jesus' words in the gospels are related to our resources and stewardship of them. Jesus not only paid His tithe to God, but also paid His taxes to the government and teaches us to do the same.[a] Though He was poor, Jesus not only fed thousands[b] but also gave us His life as a gift.[c] 2 Cor. 8:9 says, "you know the grace of our Lord Jesus Christ, that though he was rich, yet for your sake he became poor, so that you by his poverty might become rich."

Illustrated biblically: The widow[d], Tabitha[e], Barnabas[f], and the Macedonian church[g] all had this gift.

Illustrated historically: R.G. LeTourneau was a successful businessman who created his own line of earth-moving equipment in addition to some 300 inventions and hundreds of patents. As a Christian, every year he sought to increase his giving to the Lord. Eventually, after years of dedication to generosity and stewardship, his finances were a reverse tithe. Whereas most Christians live off of 90% and give 10% to God, he lived off of 10% and gave 90% TO GOD. He once humorously said, "I

---

[a] Matthew 17:24-27; 21:15-22 [b] Mark 6:41 [c] John 15:13 [d] Mark 12:42–43 [e] Acts 9:36 [f] Acts 4:34–37 [g] 2 Cor. 8:1–2

shovel out the money, and God shovels it back – but God has a bigger shovel." He did not start off wealthy, but his life seems to be an illustration of Jesus' principle regarding finances in Luke 16:10 (NLT), "If you are faithful in little things, you will be faithful in large ones. But if you are dishonest in little things, you won't be honest with greater responsibilities." The story of LeTourneau's life is not that you wait to be generous on a day that you can afford it, but that you start today and continue to be faithful as an act of worship to God.

Do you have this gift?

1. Do you tend to see the needs of others more than other people?
2. Do you enjoy giving your time, talent, and treasure to help people and ministries?
3. Do you see giving to a worthwhile project as an exciting honor and privilege?
4. Do you give to God through your local church regularly, cheerfully, and sacrificially?
5. Do you often hear people commenting that you are a generous person?
6. Do you find yourself looking for opportunities to give your money – even when no one asks?
7. Do you pray for the needs of people and organizations to be met because this is a high priority for you?
8. When you get something (e.g. a home or vacation home, car, etc.) is your first instinct to think about people you could bless by sharing it with them?
9. Do you live with a sense of deep awe at how generous God has been to you?

Faith

Place in Scripture: 1 Corinthians 12:9

Defined: Faith is the ability to envision what needs to be done and to trust God to accomplish it, even though it seems impossible to most people.

General makeup: Those with the gift of faith trust God in difficult, even impossible, situations, when others are ready to give up. These people are often visionaries who dream big dreams, pray big prayers, and attempt big things for Jesus. These people tend to be optimistic, hopeful, persevering, change-oriented, and future-focused. These people also tend to be very convincing about the truth of Scripture because they themselves are so convinced of the truth and power of God and His Word.

Warning: Sometimes, people with the gift of faith can become irresponsible and not do the things that God has asked them to do, which is disobedience. Instead, they simply say they are trusting God and praying for Him to show up and do what He has already told them to do. This is not faith, but rather folly.

Seen in Jesus' ministry: In one sense, Jesus' entire life and ministry could be summarized as one of faith because He continually and perfectly trusted in God, the Father in all things. The reason Jesus never sinned is because everything He did was in faith as Romans 14:23 says, "whatever does not proceed from faith is sin."

Illustrated biblically: Paul[a], Stephen, who was "full of faith"[b], and Jesus' mother, Mary, who trusted God to give her a child though she was a virgin.[c] Hebrews 11 also lists some Hall of Fame believers who had the gift of faith.

Illustrated historically: George Mueller (1805-1895) said, "God delights to increase the faith of his children." Mueller was a man who lived by faith and prayer alone. Charles Dickens "Oliver Twist" motivated Mueller to open the United Kingdom's first orphanage for orphaned boys and girls. He began without finances and throughout his life never asked anyone for financial support. His first orphanage began with 30 children. He would often pray with the children before meals, trusting God to somehow bring the meal they were to eat within a few minutes. Over his lifetime he cared for over 10,000 orphans, printed Bibles and books, supported over 130 missionaries, and opened a Bible college. He taught in over 30 countries on faith and prayer and died in poverty having never kept anything for himself over the course of his life.

Do you have this gift?

1. Do you view obstacles as opportunities and trust God for the impossible?
2. Do you find yourself frequently telling stories about the power of God and what you have seen Him do?
3. Do you get motivated by new ministries and new opportunities?
4. Do you find yourself feeling opposed to anyone who expresses that some thing cannot be done or accomplished?
5. Do you find other believers coming to you for hope when they face a seemingly overwhelming trial or task?
6. Do you get frustrated when you see people and ministries stuck, not making plans for the future, or not having hope and vision for something better?

---

[a] Acts 27:21-25 [b] Acts 6:5 [c] Luke 1:26-38

7. Do you tend to be less emotionally up and down than many people you know and more even keeled with a strong sense of God's faithfulness?
8. Do you have a big God and high trust in God's good and sovereign providential rule over all things?
9. Do you have an effective prayer ministry with many wonderful answers to prayers that were impossible from the human point of view?

In addition to these serving gifts, the Holy Spirit also gives speaking gifts, which we will study next.

CHAPTER 6
DISCOVERING YOUR SPIRITUAL GIFT: PART 2 (SPEAKING GIFTS)

When our oldest daughters were little, I would often sit with them on the couch and tell them we would watch whatever they wanted. As a fan of sporting events, home building shows, and pretty much anything in which bad guys are shot, it was an act of loving service to sit through countless hours of their favorite cooking and baking shows.

I cannot much cook anything beyond toast. Thankfully, I am good at ordering food from a restaurant, and my wife Grace is an amazing cook. Starting as little girls, Ashley and Alexie liked learning about new ingredients and dishes from the television, and then heading into the kitchen to cook or bake something for themselves. I was happy to be the designated taste tester sampling all their latest culinary creations.

What I gathered from my time watching cooking shows with my little ladies is that every recipe has both ingredients and measurements. The key to getting great flavors is putting the right ingredients in and doing so in the right measurement. On one occasion, I sought to help cook and, when I went to put a dash of salt in a bowl, the lid came off and we had a deluge of salt, which changed the taste of the dish from savory to seaworthy.

Ministry is a bit like cooking. God our Master Chef picks both the spiritual gift ingredients we are each given, along with the portion or measurement of each. God's recipe for each of us is unique so that our ministry contribution is uniquely flavored.

In the previous chapter, we examined serving gifts. In this chapter, we will learn about speaking gifts. In the ensuing chapter, you will learn about the more controversial and supernatural gifts.

Apostles

Place in Scripture: 1 Corinthians 12:28; Ephesians 4:11

Defined: There is much confusion regarding the spiritual gift of apostleship because there is sometimes a failure to distinguish between the office of Apostle
(*big A*) and the gift of apostle (*little a*). The office of Apostle refers to the 12 chosen
by Jesus.[a] The requirements for the office of Apostle include being an eyewitness
to the life and resurrection of Jesus.[b] Another requirement is miraculous power.[c]
Therefore, apostles do not exist today (e.g., writing books of the Bible), although the
function of their office does continue in a limited sense. For example, apostleship
in a secondary sense applies to such people as Barnabas[d], Apollos and Sosthenes[e],
Andronicus and Junias[f], James[g], and Silas and Timothy.[h] They, like apostles today,
were gifted individuals sent out to move from place to place in order to begin and
establish local churches.[i] This gift also includes the capacity to minister cross-
culturally.[k] Today, church planters and missionaries are operating out of their gift
of apostleship as well as those Christian leaders God raises up to lead and influence multiple churches and pastors. The heart of apostolic leadership is spiritual
parenting so that new generations of Christian ministry leaders are raised up in a
way that is similar to Paul with Timothy, Titus, and Onesimus, who he called "sons".
Apostolic leaders today are movement leaders with convening power to gather
Christian leaders and mobilize them for Gospel ministry.

General makeup: These people often have a number of gifts, such as evangelism,
teaching, leadership, faith, and exhortation and are motivated by difficult new
tasks.

Warning: There are two primary ways that the apostolic gift can be problematic.
One, the person with the gift is elevated by God to a level of leadership where they
are isolated and do not have sufficient care for their own well-being along with the
care for their family. Apostolic leaders tend to have such broad ministry responsibilities, public platforms that come with opposition, and pour out so much energy
that they can overextend themselves toward burnout and need godly spiritual
oversight for care. Two, the other possible error for apostolic leadership is trying to
place the care for the leader and their family in the hands of people who are not
leading at the same level of responsibility and therefore stifle or hinder the apostolic work. Often, people in this position want to be helpful but are not as helpful as

---

[a] Matthew 10:1; 19:28; 20:17; Mark 3:13–19; 6:7; 9:35; 10:32; Luke 6:12–16; 8:1; 9:1; 22:19–30;
John 6:70–71; Revelation 21:14 [b] Acts 1:21–26 [c] Acts 2:43; 5:12; 8:18; 2 Corinthians 12:12;
Hebrews 2:4 [d] Acts 14:3–4, 14 [e] 1 Corinthians 4:6–9 [f] Romans 16:7 [g] Galatians 1:19 [h] 1
Thessalonians 1:1; 2:6 [i] Acts 13:3–4 [k] Acts 10:34–35; Ephesians 3:7–8

older, more mature people who have apostolic gifting and can best relate to and provide wise counsel for others with apostolic gifting. As an example, Paul did not submit to local leadership in churches, but wrote letters to them to correct and rebuke them, which is an act of authority over them. Paul, however, submitted to others with apostolic gifting, including Peter, who was an Apostle, and James, who had apostolic gifting but was not one of the 12. This explains why Paul traveled to meet with them and submit to them.[a]

Seen in Jesus' ministry: Hebrews 3:1 says, "Therefore, holy brothers, who share in the heavenly calling, fix your thoughts on Jesus, the apostle and high priest whom we confess." Jesus also builds the Church.[b] He is the chief cornerstone of the church, upon which the foundation of the prophets and apostles is laid[c], and over which He rules as Chief Shepherd.[d]

Illustrated biblically: Paul[e]. Also, a reading of Acts shows how Paul ministered cross-culturally and planted churches. Peter also held the office of apostle.[f] Paul warning and rebuking the local elders in Ephesus was apostolic leadership.[g] Paul writing letters to rebuke local church elder teams and other leaders is also apostolic over-sight, including the rebellious[h] and religious.[i]

Illustrated historically: Hudson Taylor did not have a theological degree. He was physically small, weak and frail. He was young, a mere 19, when he began his ministry. He gave up a well-paying and respected career as a physician in England to live in poverty, obscurity and controversy in China. He refused to let money get in the way of ministry, to the point of even refusing to take an offering at meetings and funding ministry out of his own pocket. He worked at a feverish pace, at one point preaching in 58 Chinese cities in 25 days, 51 of which had never been visited by a Protestant missionary. Despite his critics, he adopted the clothing and cultural styles of China. Today, every Christian in China can trace their spiritual roots back to the efforts of Hudson Taylor.

Common errors regarding apostles: Cult leaders and erroneous teachers say that they have authority that is, in effect, equal to Scripture because they are apostles, just like those who wrote the Bible. But such people are false apostles[k] and delu-

---

[a] Acts; Galatians 1:18-19, 2:7-9 [b] Matthew 16:18; Hebrews 3:1–6 [c] Ephesians 2:20 [d] 1 Peter 5:4 [e] Romans, 1 Corinthians, 2 Corinthians, Galatians, Ephesians, Colossians, 1 Timothy, 2 Timothy, and Titus all open with Paul introducing himself as an apostle [f] Galatians 2:8; 1 Peter 1:1 [g] Acts 20:17-35 [h] 1-2 Corinthians [i] Galatians [k] 2 Corinthians 11:13; Revelation 2:2

sional "super-apostles"[a].

Do you have this gift?

1. Are you a leader of Christian leaders?
2. Do pastors and ministry leaders seek you out for wise counsel, oversight, and help?
3. Do you have a deep compassion and concern for ministry leaders and their families?
4. Can you effectively minister cross-culturally?
5. Are you called and qualified to plant a church or start a new ministry?
6. Are you a spiritual entrepreneur who likes to start something new or grow something healthier and larger?
7. Has God given you leadership and influence over multiple churches as a movement leader?
8. Can you pioneer a ministry where others have failed?
9. Do you have a longing to see Christians and various ministries and churches unified in love for the sake of the Gospel?

Teaching

Place in Scripture: Romans 12:7; 1 Corinthians 12:28

Defined: The gift of teaching is the God-given ability to understand and communicate biblical truth in a clear and relevant manner so that there is understanding and application.

General makeup: Learning, researching, communicating, and illustrating truth are qualities that an individual will manifest when exercising the gift of teaching. These people enjoy studying and learning new information and find great joy in sharing it with others. The format of teaching varies from one-on-one discipleship to formal classes, informal Bible studies, large groups, and preaching, which is a form of teaching.

Warning: Because people with the gift of teaching are strong in the realm of ideas, they can become idealistic and legalistic. People with the gift of teaching also tend to have a higher intellectual capacity than relational capacity, which means that they can become impatient and even unloving with people who are slow to process information and learn lessons. This results in a spirit that is not very teach-

---

[a] 2 Corinthians 11:5, 13; 12:11

58

able and not open to contrary opinions, which can lead to an unhealthy dogmatic disposition.

Seen in Jesus' ministry: Throughout the gospels, Jesus was commonly referred to as *Rabbi*, which means "teacher." Matthew 4:23 says that "Jesus went throughout Galilee, teaching," and Matthew 7:28–29 says that "the crowds were amazed at his [Jesus'] teaching because he taught as one who had authority, and not as their teachers of the law."

Illustrated biblically: Aquila and Priscilla[a], Paul[b], pastors and ministry leaders[c], Timothy[d], and godly women[e] all demonstrated the gift of teaching.

Illustrated historically: John Calvin (1509-1564) was one of the greatest and most significant teachers in all of history. Converted around age 23, he published his now famous "Institutes for the Christian Religion" at the age of 26. It was the first and most thorough and significant outline of what has come to be known as Calvinistic theology. At age 28, Calvin settled in Geneva and soon established schools with intense academic teaching throughout the city. He later founded a university for more academic instruction. Calvin's passion for teaching has made him the father of modern education in numerous countries, including America. Wherever Calvinism spread, it brought with it schools and teaching. Calvin promoted education for everyone, which was a revolutionary concept that has now become a pattern throughout the world. By the turn of this century, his impact was clearly seen worldwide. In pagan nations, such as China and India, with little exposure to the Word of God, the literacy rate ranged from 0-20%. Roman Catholic countries ranged from 40-60%. In Protestant influenced countries, the literacy rate ranged from 94-99.9%. In America, the first 123 colleges and universities had Christian origins that were directly influenced by the teachings of John Calvin.

Do you have this gift?

1. Do you enjoy studying and researching?
2. Do you enjoy imparting biblical truth to others?
3. Do others come to you for insight into Scripture?
4. When you teach, do people "get it"?
5. When you see someone confused in their understanding of the Bible, do you feel a responsibility to speak to them about it?

---

[a] Acts 18:26 [b] Acts 19:8–10; 20:20; Colossians 1:28; 1 Timothy 2:7 [c] 1 Timothy 3:2; 5:17 [d] 1 Timothy 4:11,13; 6:2 [e] Titus 2:2–4

6. Do you enjoy speaking to various sizes of groups about biblical issues you have strong convictions about?

7. Do people seek you out for answers to their questions and help with biblical and theological issues?

8. Does your study of subjects tend to go "deeper" than most people because you are unusually curious?

Evangelism

<u>Place in Scripture:</u> Ephesians 4:11

<u>Defined:</u> The gift of evangelism is the ability and desire to boldly and clearly communicate the gospel of Jesus Christ so that non-Christians can become Christians.

<u>General makeup:</u> Evangelists often care passionately about lost people and have a strong desire to see them meet Jesus. They feel compassion for the lost and seek to earnestly understand their questions and doubts so that they can provide a compelling answer. An evangelist often prefers being with people in the culture rather than hanging out with Christians in the church.

<u>Warning:</u> Sometimes evangelists care so much about people outside the church who are non-Christians that they are less loving than they should be for Christians who are in the church. This can include a judgmental spirit for people who are not as zealous to reach lost people.

<u>Seen in Jesus' ministry:</u> Luke 19:10 says that "the Son of Man came to seek and to save what was lost." People accused Jesus of being "a friend of tax collectors and 'sinners'" because He had many evangelistic relationships with sinful people.[a] The entire point of Jesus coming from Heaven to earth was to be an evangelist and to "seek and save the lost".[b]

<u>Illustrated biblically:</u> The Apostle Paul gave his life to evangelism and public ministry – he walked an average of 20 miles a day for nearly a decade, was single and without a wife, was poor, worked side jobs, was sent to prison and left for dead multiple times, and preached a message that led to both revivals and riots. Through it all, he would not stop preaching the Gospel because, as an evangelist, he was completely devoted to reaching people and planting churches. Philip[c], and Timothy[d], also have this gift. The first, and perhaps greatest, evangelist in the New Testament was the sinful Samaritan women Jesus met with at a well in John 4 who went in

---

[a] Matthew 11:19 [b] Luke 19:10 [c] Acts 21:8 [d] 2 Timothy 4:5

to town to tell everyone about Jesus so that a great evangelistic revival broke out among some of the most lost pagan people in the ancient world.

Illustrated historically: George Whitefield (1714–1770) began preaching at the age of 24 and is arguably the greatest preacher America has ever produced. He preached 18,000 sermons to over 10,000,000 people during the Great Awakening. He planted 150 churches in New England, New York, New Jersey, Pennsylvania, and Maryland. He preached in open air with crowds as large as 30,000 people at a time. Amazingly, he preached to such crowds without a microphone and would cough up blood from the strain on his throat. It is estimated that most Americans heard him preach at least once as he addressed perhaps 10,000,000 hearers in person before modern media. His farewell sermon at Boston Common drew more people than Boston's entire population and was the largest crowd ever gathered in America up to that time. Whitefield once said, "God forbid that I should travel with anybody a quarter of an hour without speaking of Christ to them."

Do you have this gift?

1. Do you enjoy being with non-Christians and sharing the Gospel?
2. Are you able to effectively communicate to non-Christians in a way they can understand?
3. Does a person's conversion bring you profound joy?
4. Do you feel frustrated when you haven't shared your faith for a while?
5. Do you enjoy teaching other Christians how to share their faith?
6. Do you find it easy to direct a conversation toward the topic of Jesus Christ?
7. Do you find it rather easy to have conversations about God with non-Christians that most Christians would find a bit awkward or uncomfortable?
8. When you think of lost people you know, is your heart a bit like Jesus, who wept over the lost people in His city of Jerusalem?

Shepherding/Care

Place in Scripture: Ephesians 4:11

Defined: In one sense, pastoring is the office reserved for those who meet the Biblical criteria.[a] In another sense, there is a pastoral gift also commonly known as shepherding or Christian counseling that God gives to people in the church beyond those who hold an official leadership position in the church. These people protect,

---

[a] 1 Timothy 3:1–7; Titus 1:5–9

guide, counsel, and disciple other people.

General makeup: The person with a pastoral gifting has a love for people that compels them to meet with people to care for them and guide them with Biblical instruction. People with this gift find great joy in seeing people mature in their faith and overcome besetting sin and discouragement so that they are healthy and living out the fruit of the Spirit.

Warning: In ministry, there are three kinds of relationships. Personal relationships are people we draw close, trust as peers, and do life with. Professional relationships are those we have with people like doctors, lawyers, and accountants where we have to schedule an appointment and pay them for their services. Pastoral relationships are difficult because they are between the personal and professional. People with the gift of shepherding/care can treat everyone like a personal friend, lose healthy boundaries, and develop unhealthy and even co-dependent relationships if not wise and careful. Worse still, a soul tie can form, which is an unhealthy spiritual relationship that is the equivalent of an unhealthy physical or emotional relationship where a ministry leader and their followers become so spiritually intertwined that the relationship is ungodly in the name of Christian love.

Seen in Jesus' ministry: Jesus is called the "good Shepherd"[a] and the "Chief Shepherd".[b] Also, the Bible gives us snapshots of Jesus sitting with people to pastor them, such as His interaction with the Samaritan woman at the well in John 4.

Illustrated biblically: At the end of his letter to the Romans, Paul provides a long list of men and women who were doing good shepherding work caring for the people in the church.[c] Paul does this same thing at the end of other New Testament letters as well. Since he is not present, he names the people who are present to help shepherd the flock.[d] Throughout the New Testament, a married couple named Priscilla and Aquila are repeatedly seen doing pastoral care for people in their home[e], including raising up Apollos, who became a powerful preacher.[f]

Illustrated historically: Puritan Richard Baxter lived from 1615 to 1691. He entered vocational ministry at the age of 23 without any formal education. He pastored in a small English town of 2000 people. He took these "ignorant, rude and reveling people" and turned them into a worshipping church of 1000 people. He viewed

---

[a] John 10:11–14; 13:20; 1 Peter 2:25 [b] 1 Peter 5:4 [c] Romans 16:3-16 [d] 1 Corinthians 16; Colossians 4; 2 Timothy 4 [e] Acts 18:2, 18:18: Romans 16:3; 1 Corinthians 16:19 [f] Acts 18:24-28

teaching as his primary task and focused on the basics of the Christian faith. Each year he would personally visit the homes of each member of his congregation and did a great amount of counseling. He held a weekly pastor's forum for discussion and prayer in which he encouraged and trained numerous pastors. His gifted training of other pastors culminating in his classic book, "The Reformed Pastor", one of his 200 writings.

Do you have this gift?

1. Do you have a deep love for people that compels you to care for them?
2. Do you enjoy meeting with people to listen to their life story and provide them biblical counsel?
3. When you hear that someone is hurting, is your first instinct to try and meet with them to be of help?
4. Are you able to point out sin and folly in someone's life in a loving way that they receive as helpful?
5. Do you enjoy meeting with Christians to help them mature in their faith?
6. Do people pursue you for wise counsel and instruction?
7. Do you find yourself meeting with people regularly to help them take the next steps on their faith walk?
8. Do you find great joy in seeing people heal up, grow, mature, and move forward in life and having a front row seat to witness that work of the Holy Spirit?

Encouragement

Place in Scripture: Romans 12:8

Defined: The gift of encouragement (also called the gift of exhortation) involves motivating, encouraging, and consoling others so they mature in their walk with Jesus. To encourage someone is to literally pour courage into them to strengthen and sustain them.

General makeup: Christians with this gift have an unusual sensitivity for and are attracted to those who are discouraged or struggling. As a result, people tend to pursue them for healing words, gracious truth, and compassionate counsel. These people also tend to have a high degree of patience and optimism. They may have a knack for one-on-one relationships and prefer working with an individual or small group.

Warning: People with this gift can be so hopeful for someone that they lack discernment in seeing evil and even folly in others. These people can also struggle with conflict and having to say and do hard things, because they know that others will not approve of their leadership. People with this gift can also have a hard time with truth tellers, direct leadership styles, and those who are more prophetic and discerning because their methods seem less loving and patient.

Seen in Jesus' ministry: Jesus told us to love even our enemies and do good to them[a], and exhorted people to "leave your life of sin"[b]. We are told that, "there is... encouragement in Christ".[c]

Illustrated biblically: Barnabas, whose name means "Son of Encouragement"[d], encouraged Paul[e] and John Mark.[f] Paul had this gift[g] as did Judas and Silas.[h] Paul says that the Bible is written so that "through endurance and through the encouragement of the Scriptures we might have hope" because our god is "the God of endurance and encouragement".[i] Lastly, the New Testament repeatedly encourages Christians to "encourage one another".[k]

Illustrated historically: The Great Reformer Martin Luther sought to purify the church and, in doing so, split the church into Catholicism and Protestantism. Involved in continual opposition and controversies, his life was in constant danger, his friends rejected and opposed him, his church rejected him, and as a result, Luther struggled mightily with deep depression. The ill health of his final 10 years further contributed to his depression. His wife, Katherine, was a gifted encourager who strengthened, supported and counseled her husband as he spearheaded the Reformation. Without her gift of encouragement, it is doubtful Luther would have had the strength and will to continue pressing forward with his calling from God. The couple lived in great poverty with great responsibility. They had three boys and three girls during their first nine years of marriage. Tragically, one daughter died at the age of 13 months and another at 13 years in the arms of her devastated father. By all accounts, Katherine was a wonderful mother and Martin a loving and fun father who spent his evenings playing music for his children and teaching them the Bible, which was a welcome and joyous diversion from his busy and stressful life. Martin's old 40-room monastery became their home, and Katie quickly went to work cleaning the bachelor pad, including throwing out the straw bed Luther had

---

[a] Luke 6:27–35 [b] John 8:11 [c] Philippians 2:1 [d] Acts 4:36 [e] Acts 9:27 [f] Acts 15:39 [g] Acts 14:21–22; 16:40; 20:1 [h] 15:31–32 [i] Romans 15:4-5 [k] Romans 1:12; 1 Corinthians 14:3, 14:31; 1 Thessalonians 4:18, 5:11, 5:14; 2 Thessalonians 3:12

not changed in more than a year, decorating the home, planting a garden for fresh food, changing Martin's diet to nurse him to health and help overcome his legendary flatulence problem, and growing herbs, as she was a bit of a naturopath. Their home was bustling with activity. Martin was constantly studying and publishing to fuel the Protestant Reformation, preaching and teaching, working on translating the entire Bible into German, traveling, and keeping up a vast correspondence with ministers across many nations. Katherine often sat with Martin as he wrote letters, for they frequently included sections about what Katherine was doing at the time and the greetings she sent. Their home was constantly filled, and as many as 25 people lived with them at any one time, not to mention the 11 orphans they sheltered. Dinners there often fed more than 100 people. Something that helped them learn to live together in love was their willingness to dish out and take a joke. For example, when one would start to nag, the other would commonly retort that perhaps a little prayer should occur before "preaching a sermon." His letters often teased her, but Katherine certainly could hold her own. Martin often struggled with severe depression, and it was very difficult to pull him out of his funk. But Katherine found creative ways to do so. On one occasion she dressed up like a grieving widow in black mourning attire and met Martin at their door upon his return home. "Are you going to a funeral?" he asked. "No," she replied, "but since you act as though God is dead, I wanted to join you in the mourning." Luther quickly recovered! Through their years together, the Luthers built a genuine friendship. This is easily noticed in the letters we have from Martin to his wife. His favorite title for her was "Lord Katie." He also called her his "dear rib," "Sir Katie," "the empress," "my true love," "my sweetheart," and "a gift of God." When he suffered from catarrh, kidney stones, constipation, insomnia, dizziness, and a buzzing – "not a buzzing but a roll of thunder" – in his head, she nursed him back to health. When he would fall into his frequent bouts with severe depression, she would hold him, pray for him, comfort him, and read Scripture to him. She drove the wagon, looked after their fields and gardens, purchased and pastured cattle, brewed beer, rented horses, sold linen, helped edit his writings, prepared meals, kept house, raised kids, entertained guests, and was often awake by 4:00 a.m. and working until 9:00 p.m. She was such an incredibly hard worker that Martin had to frequently urge her to relax and even offered to pay her to sit down and read her Bible. She reportedly had a keen theological mind and often sat with Martin and visiting theologians to discuss and debate theology—something unusual for a woman in that day. The tenderness with which Martin spoke of his wife increased throughout their marriage. He wrote, "I am a happy husband and may God continue to send me happiness, from that most gracious woman, my best of wives." As their loving friendship grew, his perspective matured as suggested by statements such as, "The greatest gift of grace a man can have is a pious, God-fearing, home-loving wife, whom he can trust with all his goods, body, and life itself, as well as having her as the mother of his children." After preaching what would be his final sermon, Martin died at the age of 62, while away from his beloved Katie. In his will he said, "My Katherine has always been a gentle, pious and faithful wife to me, has loved me dearly."

Do you have this gift?

1. Do you find yourself attracted to help people who are fearful, struggling, or discouraged?
2. Do you find that you often have more courage than most people in tough situations and people borrow courage from you?
3. Do people seek you out for advice and encouragement?
4. Do you enjoy walking with someone through difficulties?
5. Are you attracted to those who are hurting and needy?
6. Are you patient with people?
7. Would you rather speak personally with someone about their problems rather than send them to someone else for help?
8. Do you find it easy to express joy in the presence of those who are suffering?

Leadership

Place in Scripture: Romans 12:8

Defined: The spiritual gift of leadership is found in people who have a clear, significant vision from God and are able to communicate it publicly or privately in such a way that they influence others to pursue that vision.

General makeup: These people tend to gravitate toward the "point position" in a ministry. Others tend to have trust and confidence in their abilities. They best serve others by leading them. They tend to operate with a strong sense of destiny.

Warning: Sometimes a leader can be so confident in their own abilities that they do not consider the input of others and, as a result, make bad decisions from an unhealthy degree of independence. Some leaders like to be over others but do not like to have others in authority over them. Wise leaders seek godly, healthy, and wise oversight to help them be even better leaders as they follow leaders over them. Because a leader is often out front, they can struggle with feeling lonely and discouraged by not only calling the shots but taking the shots and they need to constantly seek wise counsel and care to remain holy, healthy, and hopeful. Lastly, leadership begins with yourself, and your family, and some people want to lead in ministry without having their priorities in order as leadership starts at home.

Seen in Jesus' ministry: Jesus was such a gifted leader that in His day thousands followed Him and today billions follow Him as the greatest leader who has ever lived. When Jesus recruited others by saying "follow me", He was establishing Himself clearly as the Leader of all other Christian leaders as Matthew's Gospel repeatedly reveals.[a]

Illustrated biblically: Examples abound, including Abraham, Moses, Joshua, David, Daniel, Josiah, Paul, Peter, and James. In some ways, the Bible is largely about the work of the Holy Spirit for, in, and through human leaders.

Illustrated historically: Athanasius is widely regarded as one of the most important theological leaders in the history of the Christian faith. He was born between AD 296 and 298 and at some point, early in life, came to love Jesus Christ and God and spent a great deal of time reading the Bible. As a young man, he was discovered by the prominent theologian Alexander who hired him to serve as an assistant. Another Christian theologian named Arius was roughly 40 years Athanasius' senior and was born around AD 256. In AD 319, Arius sparked a vigorous theological debate that gripped the church for some 60 years. The Arian controversy attacked three of the most important Christian doctrines. First, it denied that Jesus Christ is eternal and existed prior to his incarnation. Two, it denied that Jesus is fully God. Three, it denied the doctrine of the Trinity, which states that there is one God in three persons – Father, Son, and Spirit. The Arian controversy was causing great division both in the church and the Roman Empire, so Constantine called a council in Nicaea in AD 325 in an effort to mediate the conflict. The Council of Nicaea was attended by approximately three hundred bishops as well as other Christian leaders who were not bishops, such as Arius and Athanasius. Many of the bishops in attendance bore the marks of their conflict, such as scars on their bodies, and one bishop was missing a hand and another missing an eye from persecution over the issue. The debate raged from May until August. The Nicene Creed resulted from

---

[a] Matthew 4:19, 8:22, 9:9, 10:38, 16:24, 19:21, 19:28, 20:29

the Council at Nicaea and confirmed that Jesus Christ is eternally God and the second member of the Trinity. This document has served as the definition for Christian orthodoxy in every generation since and explains why many refer to Athanasius as the "father of orthodoxy." His book "On the Incarnation", which he penned while still in his twenties, remains one of the most important theological books ever written because it cogently and biblically argues that Jesus Christ is eternally God and the second member of the Trinity who became a man to redeem men from their sin. Although a man of slight build and gracious demeanor, Athanasius fought boldly for his Trinitarian God and Lord Jesus Christ. Members of his churches were murdered, including men who were hung and women who were slaughtered. Athanasius' enemies routinely brought false charges against him; they ran him out of town into exile on five occasions, for a total of 17 of his 45 years as bishop. Pastor Athanasius was dearly loved by his people and was warmly welcomed by them each time he returned from exile. He died in AD 373 as an elderly man, loving pastor, and pastor to fellow pastors. Eight years after his death, in AD 381, Athanasius was finally vindicated when his doctrines about Jesus Christ were officially confirmed as biblical orthodoxy at the Council of Constantinople, some 60 years after the Arian controversy erupted. Though he was not a bishop, Athanasius emerged as the leader of Christian orthodoxy. His leadership began not from his position, but by God elevating him during a time of crisis to lead Christianity away from heresy and into orthodoxy.

Do you have this gift?

1. Do others have confidence in your ability to lead?
2. Do you enjoy being the "final voice" or the one with the overall responsibility for the direction and success of a group or organization?
3. When a difficult situation arises, do others look to you for input and leadership?
4. Do you usually take leadership in a group where none exists?
5. Do you find yourself carrying burdens for people and things that others do not?
6. Do you find leadership enjoyable rather than frustrating and difficult?
7. Do others look to you to make the major decisions for a group or organization?
8. Do you tend to have clear vision for a better future that others agree with and rally around?

9. Are you able to bring other leaders with giftings different than yours together to accomplish tasks?

Wisdom

<u>Place in Scripture:</u> 1 Corinthians 12:8

<u>Defined:</u> The gift of wisdom is the ability to have insight into people and situations that is not obvious to the average person, combined with an understanding of what to do and how to do it. It is the ability to not only see, but also apply the principles of God's Word to the practical matters of life by the "Spirit of wisdom".[a]

<u>General makeup:</u> These people often have an ability to synthesize biblical truth and apply it to people's lives so that they make good choices and avoid foolish mistakes. These people today function well as coaches, counselors, and consultants. They tend to be very practical about what to do and not do. Whereas teachers love books of the Bible like Romans, people with the gift of wisdom like books of the Bible like Proverbs.

<u>Warning:</u> Sometimes people with the gift of wisdom see things differently, find creative solutions, and like to be agents of change. In their shadow side, this can lead to a spirit of criticism, pointing out problems without offering any solutions, and becoming negative and jaded. This can also lead to a desire for new ideas and perspectives that can lead into false teaching and an attraction to things that go beyond the Scriptures in the name of being innovative, groundbreaking, or reforming. Romans 1:22 says, "Claiming to be wise, they became fools..." Satan's first temptation was to become "wise" by rebelling against God's authority. Lastly, some people with the gift of wisdom give wise counsel to others but do not apply it to their own lives, which is hypocrisy.

<u>Seen in Jesus' ministry:</u> Luke 2:40–52 says that Jesus was "filled with wisdom" as a boy and "grew in wisdom" as a young man so that the scholars of His day were "amazed at his understanding." Crowds who heard Jesus teach said, "What's this wisdom that has been given him".[b] In Matthew 12:42, Jesus said that He was wiser than Solomon. And in Luke 21:15, Jesus said, "I will give you words and wisdom." We are also told that Jesus is the "wisdom of God".[c]

<u>Illustrated biblically:</u> Throughout the Old Testament[d] and New Testament[e], leaders were chosen because they were "wise". Joshua[f], Solomon[g], and Daniel[h] all have this

---

[a] Ephesians 1:17 [b] Mark 6:2 [c] 1 Cor. 1:24, 30 [d] Deut. 4:6 [e] 1 Cor. 6:5 [f] Deut. 34:9; 1 Kings 5:7; 2 Chron. 2:12 [g] 1 Kings 3:5–28 [h] Daniel 1:17–20; 2:19–23

gift. There is an entire genre of literature in the Bible called "wisdom literature" that includes Psalms, Proverbs, Ecclesiastes, Job, and James.

Illustrated historically: A.W. Tozer was born into a poor home in the hills of western Pennsylvania. Forced by his home to forfeit education, Tozer entered the ministry without either high school or college training. Tozer came to Christ at age 15, after hearing a lay preacher speaking at a street meeting at Akron, Ohio. He went on to a lifetime of faithful pastoral ministry. Thousands regularly listened to his preaching on the Moody Bible Institute radio station. He became a very gifted writer and spent a number of years editing the *Alliance Witness* magazine. Tozer's only education was years of diligent study with a constant prayerful seeking of the mind of God, often for hours on end, kneeling and asking the Holy Spirit for wisdom in prayer with his Bible open. For example, when he desired to understand the works of Shakespeare, he read them through on his knees, asking God to help him understand their meaning. Tozer wrote dozens of books, including "The Pursuit of God" while on his knees. With no teacher but the Holy Spirit and good books, Tozer became a theologian, a scholar, and a master craftsman in the use of the English language. His teaching was intensely practical as he taught how to integrate deep theological truths into practical daily living. He has become a world-renowned Christian teacher because of his supernatural wisdom from the Holy Spirit.

Do you have this gift?

1. Do you have a pattern of making wise decisions for your life and family that helps you give wise counsel to others?
2. Do you seek wise counsel from people wiser than you?
3. When studying God's Word, do you find that you discover the meaning and its implications before others do?
4. Do you seem to understand things about God's Word which other believers with the same background and experience don't seem to know?
5. When studying the Bible, do you find yourself moving toward practical actions to apply what is taught so that you can study for transformation and not just information?
6. Do you get frustrated when people make foolish decisions that damage their quality of life because you know what they should have done instead?
7. Do you find that when people have important decisions to make, they come to you for prayer and biblical counsel?
8. Do you find that, when you counsel people, God the Spirit gives you wisdom

to share with them from Scripture, which they accept as God's truth to them through you?

Knowledge

Place in Scripture: 1 Corinthians 12:8

Defined: The word of knowledge is the ability to research, remember, and make effective use of a variety of information on a number of diverse subjects.

General makeup: These people love to study and learn and are not content with a surface-level knowledge of topics. They are compelled to conduct thorough research and compile their findings so that others can benefit from their long hours of focused study. People with this spiritual gift love God with "all [their] mind".[a]

Warning: They can often become proud because "knowledge puffs up".[b]

Seen in Jesus' ministry: Throughout His ministry, Jesus frequently quoted the Old Testament Scriptures from memory because He had committed Himself to studying Scripture so faithfully. Jesus also rebuked the scholars of His day because they studied the Bible but failed to love Him, which is the purpose of all study.[c]

Illustrated biblically: The Bible is clear that a healthy respect for God is the beginning of wisdom so that we are humble enough to learn from God.[d] Knowledge is mentioned in Proverbs more than any book of the Bible because it is foundational to wise living. Paul's prayer for the church in Colossians 1:9-10 is that "you may be filled with the knowledge of his will in all spiritual wisdom and understanding... increasing in the knowledge of God..." Ezra[e], Solomon[f], and Timothy[g] all had the spiritual gift of knowledge. The Apostle Paul had the gift of knowledge as he was fluent in Hebrew, Aramaic, Greek, and possibly Latin. In his letters, most likely from memory, he has over 100 Old Testament quotations, in addition to numerous themes and references.

Illustrated historically: Blaise Pascal (1623-1662) was a French scholar who's short 39 years produced brilliant insight into a variety of academic disciplines. Pascal was masterful in mathematics, probability science, physics, and philosophy. He was considered a child prodigy in literary circles. He wrote his first groundbreaking scientific essay on conic sections based upon synthetic projective geometry around the age of 17. He created the first working barometer, first working calculator to help his father with tax computations, laid the academic foundation for

---

[a] Mark 12:29–30 [b] 1 Corinthians 8:1 [c] John 5:39 [d] Proverbs 1:7 [e] Ezra 7:10 [f] Ecclesiastes 1:13; 7:25; 8:9 [g] 2 Timothy 2:15

differential and integral calculus, and conducted the basic research on vacuums and hydraulics. While experimenting, Pascal invented the syringe and created the hydraulic. He also had a profound personal love for God and published one of the finest apologetically defenses of the Christian faith, *Penseés*. Sadly, that book is not his completed works but rather the various thoughts he had collected in hopes of writing an entire book. In it, the brilliant mind taught that a relationship with God must contain not merely information about God for the mind but experience of God for the heart. His religious philosophy was foundational for later philosophers such as Jean-Jacques Rousseau and the Existentialist school of philosophy. Pascal is one of the most towering, brilliant minds despite his few years on the earth. He deeply and passionately loved Jesus Christ and saw his entire mental life as worshipping God with all his mind as an incredibly godly example for all Christian scholars with the spiritual gift of knowledge.

Do you have this gift?

1. Do you love to study?
2. Do you have a good memory that retains and compiles lots of information?
3. Are you able to categorize and synthesize information in ways that most people cannot?
4. Have others frequently pointed out your ability to know and understand God's Word?
5. Are you a mentally curious person who finds new things to learn a fun challenge?
6. Do people often come to you with difficult problems and questions from the Bible, seeking your insight because they know you will have the answer or will find it?
7. In studying God's Word, have you found that new insights and understanding of difficult subjects come easy to you?
8. Are you frustrated when you hear bad teaching from someone who has not done their homework?
9. Does information, lies, and untruth bother you at a profoundly deep level?

In addition to these speaking gifts, the Holy Spirit also gives supernatural gifts, which are the most controversial, as we will study next.

CHAPTER 7
DISCOVERING YOUR SPIRITUAL GIFT: PART 3 (SIGN GIFTS)

When I was a little boy, God began a tremendous turn in my life and our family when he healed my mom. My mom was raised Catholic, but then started participating in a charismatic renewal that swept through numerous Christian denominations bringing people together for worship and prayer from various churches. My mom had a recurring health problem that made her life painful. So, she asked for prayer and some women filled with the Holy Spirit prayed for her and my mom was healed, never to struggle with that issue again.

Growing up, I did not know the Lord. What I was sure of, however, was that there was a God, and my mom knew Him. Her prayers were answered, and she had supernatural revelations and actions from God in her life that she told us kids about. My mom came to know the Lord and grew in her relationship with the Lord through power. To this day, her relationship with the Lord includes a lot of supernatural elements.

My conversion to Jesus Christ was less about power, and more about persuasion. I had a lot of questions and objections about Christianity, interest in other philosophies and spiritualities, and needed answers. God in His providence connected me with a group of strong and learned Christians at a state university of all places. This included a philosophy professor who loved the Lord, and a pastor with what I think is a PhD in Hebrew. These men, and others, patiently and kindly answered all of my questions and objections. Once I came to saving faith in Christ, every season since has been filled with supernatural activity – both from the Lord and from the Enemy.

Jesus used both persuasion and power during His earthly ministry and continues to use both to this day. His words said He is God. His works showed He is God. In John 10:36b-39, He says, "Why then do you accuse me of blasphemy because I said, 'I am God's Son'? Do not believe me unless I do what my Father does. But if I do it, even though you do not believe me, believe the miracles, that you may know and understand that the Father is in me, and I in the Father." Again they tried to seize him, but he escaped their grasp." Jesus' rule over the physical world shows Him as Creator God. Roughly 40 miracles He performed are reported in the four gospels. In Mark's Gospel, roughly one-third of all the verses deal with miracles. The Jewish Talmud, and later Celsus, who opposed Christianity, charged that Jesus "practiced magic." The noted Jewish historian Josephus also reported that Jesus was "a doer of wonderful works." Jesus' resurrection is also the greatest miracle in world history, never repeated by anyone. Jesus did so many miracles that the Bible only records some of them. John 20:30, 21:25 says, "Now Jesus did many other signs in the presence of the disciples, which are not written...Were every one of them to be written, I suppose that the world itself could not contain the books that would be written." The reason why the miracles recorded in the Bible were chosen is for the purpose of helping people believe in Jesus as God as John 20:31 says, "these are written so that you may believe that Jesus is the Christ, the Son of God, and that by believing you may have life in his name."

Biblical Christianity is Supernatural Christianity

In another book I wrote with my wife Grace called *Win Your War*, we establish the necessity of embracing the supernatural to be a Bible-believing Christian and we will summarize portions of that book in this one to lay the groundwork for understanding the supernatural spiritual gifts. You cannot believe God's Word or understand God's world unless you embrace the supernatural. From beginning to end, the Bible is about an unseen realm as real as the visible world. Faith is required to believe in beings as real as we are who live in a world as real as ours and travel between these worlds, impacting and affecting human history and our daily lives. As a result, everything is spiritual, and nothing is secular. What happens in the invisible world affects what happens in the visible world, and vice versa. Furthermore, everyone is both a physical being with a body that is seen and a spiritual being with a soul that is unseen. Spiritual warfare is like gravity – it exists whether or not you believe in it, and it affects you every moment of every day.

Christianity has largely downplayed, if not dismissed, this truth for hundreds of years. Other than Pentecostal and Charismatic Christians, many denominations and their seminaries seeking to win the approval of worldly scholarship were too influenced by the rationalism, naturalism, and skepticism of modernity that corresponds in large part with the history of America.

Rationalism disbelieved most anything that could not be seen through a telescope or microscope and believed only that which could be proven through the scientific method of testing and re-testing. This led to naturalism, a worldview that suggests all we have is the material and not the spiritual. The result was skepticism of anything spiritual, and eventually atheism and the denial of God altogether.

As this worldly thinking overtook academia, belief in such things as angels, demons, healing, and prophecy was looked down on as primitive and naïve. Surely humanity had evolved beyond such archaic views. Christian colleges and seminaries seeking approval and accreditation eventually downplayed or dismissed the supernatural parts of the Scriptures.

On the flip side, much Christian teaching on the demonic in recent years that does believe in the supernatural is combined with wild speculation and sensationalism not anchored to sound biblical principles. As a result, some Christians find talk of Satan and demons to be distracting from the glory of God and sound Bible teaching. The result is that, sure, we give a nod to the big supernatural issues like Jesus' virgin conception and bodily resurrection, but beyond that many Christians live as skeptics rather than seekers of the supernatural.

Thankfully, biblical scholarship is doing an incredible job connecting persuasion and power with detailed academic study of the supernatural. Michael Heiser's book *The Unseen Realm* is a personal favorite, along with the two-volume set called *Miracles* by Craig Keener where he spends over 1000 pages detailing miracles with a focus on the Gospels and Acts.

The supernatural parts of the Bible are often referred to as "signs". When you are driving down the road and see a sign pointing you in a direction, the goal is to direct your future toward a destination. Similarly, miracles and other supernatural events in this life are signs pointing to the Kingdom of God ruled by King Jesus intended to direct your future toward this eternal destination.

God Creates, Satan Counterfeits

Biblical Christianity requires black-and-white thinking because it is dualistic. From beginning to end, the Bible is thoroughly categorical: Satan and God, demons and angels, sin and holiness, world and Kingdom, pride and humility, idolatry and worship, lies and truth, wolves and shepherds, non-Christians and Christians, damnation and salvation, Spirit-filled and demon possessed, hell and Heaven.

An exhaustive list could fill a book, but you get the point. The Bible makes clear distinctions and judgments between opposed categories. Discernment is literally testing the spirit at work behind the supernatural to see if it is created by God or a counterfeit from Satan. This is what 1 John 4:1 intends saying, "Beloved, do not believe every spirit, but test the spirits to see whether they are from God, for many false prophets have gone out into the world."

Jesus our Good Shepherd uses some imagery that is echoed throughout the Bible. Leaders of God's people are to be like shepherds, God's people are like sheep and supposed to live together like a flock, and the shepherds need to be on guard to protect the sheep from wolves. Wolves include both human and demonic beings who come to ravage flocks and sheep. Discernment is the ability to see the wolves to protect the sheep.

Throughout this chapter, we are working from binary thinking and the premise that what God creates, Satan counterfeits. Satan creates nothing, but he does counterfeit, corrupt, and co-opt what God creates, "The coming of the lawless one is based on Satan's working, with all kinds of false miracles, signs, and wonders".[a]

The book of Exodus is a case study between God creating and Satan counterfeiting. Egypt is the manifestation of the kingdom of darkness counterfeiting the Kingdom of God; Pharaoh is the counterfeit Jesus, worshipped as the son of the gods. Pagan priests counterfeit the real priests of God and perform counterfeit miracles to copy the mighty works of God. Exodus records 40 years of this battle between the godly and genuine and the corrupt and counterfeit during the most active, supernatural period of history recorded in Scripture. The plotline of Exodus is nothing less than a cosmic continuation of the battle in Heaven. Moses and Aaron represented God; Pharaoh and Egypt represented Satan. The stage for the showdown between God and the demon gods was set when Pharaoh asked, "Who is the LORD, that I should obey his voice and let Israel go? I do not know the LORD, and moreover, I will not let Israel go."[b]

One big lesson learned from Exodus is that God's people are not to be vaguely spiritual, but very Spirit-filled. Jesus warns about demonic supernatural counterfeits saying in Mark 13:21-23, "if anyone says to you, 'Look, here is the Christ!' or 'Look, there he is!' do not believe it. For false christs and false prophets will arise

---

[a] 2 Thessalonians 2:9 (CSB) [b] Exodus 5:2

and perform signs and wonders, to lead astray, if possible, the elect. But be on guard; I have told you all things beforehand." Supernatural signs and wonders can be so intriguing that people actually start seeking them rather than the Lord which opens them up to demonic counterfeits. Jesus warned in Luke 11:29-30, "When the crowds were increasing, he began to say, 'This generation is an evil generation. It seeks for a sign, but no sign will be given to it except the sign of Jonah. For as Jonah became a sign to the people of Nineveh, so will the Son of Man be to this generation.'" The point is simply this, God's people should not seek signs and wonders. God's people should seek God and expect signs and wonders to follow them as the follow God. We will now examine this very thing in the form of miracles, prophecy, healing, and tongues. Because these are such controversial matters, we will devote more time to explaining each of these supernatural spiritual gifts than we did the serving and speaking gifts and not focus as much on their historical practice for the sake of brevity. Perhaps one day I might write entire short books on each of these subjects to explore them further, but for now the hope is a robust introduction to the supernatural spiritual gifts.

Miracles

Place in Scripture: 1 Corinthians 12:9

Defined: The gift of miracles is the ability to call on God to do supernatural acts that reveal His power by special moments of divine anointing from God the Holy Spirit.

General makeup: People with the gift of miracles see God show up in extraordinary ways from daily little events to major public displays. In these moments, there is an overriding of the natural laws, which govern the universe, and God shows up to reveal His sovereign rule as Creator over creation. Examples from the Bible include seeing demons cast out of people, nature obeying God's authority, people being healed, animals and objects speaking and acting in extraordinary ways, divine appearances of angels and other divine beings, and the dead being raised. Obviously, these sorts of things are uncommon and do not happen regularly, otherwise they would not be viewed as miraculous.

Seen in Jesus' ministry: Acts 2:22 says Jesus performed many miracles and John 20:20–31 says that Jesus' many miracles were to prove He was God. Jesus commanded nature[a], cast out demons[b], walked on water[c], turned water into wine[d], and

---

[a] Mark 4:35–41 [b] Mark 5:1–13; Matthew 12: 22 [c] Mark 6:45–51 [d] John 2:1-11

fed over 5,000 people with one boy's lunch.[a]

Illustrated biblically: The apostles did "many miraculous signs"[b], Stephen did "great" miracles[c], and Paul did "extraordinary" miracles at Ephesus.[d] Also, Paul cast out demons[e], God blinded a sorcerer for Paul[f], and there were many miracles surrounding the ministries of Moses, Elijah, and Elisha.

Miracles theologically:

The new covenant church of Jesus Christ began with the pouring out of the Spirit of God on the day of Pentecost. What happened that day Acts 2:1-4 says, "came from heaven" as the unseen realm flooded and invaded the world and included "a sound like a mighty rushing wind" (Spirit of God) as "tongues as of fire appeared to them and rested on each one of them. And they were all filled with the Holy Spirit."

Just as your body is united with two parts – the physical seen and the spiritual unseen – so too is our world one reality that is a combination of two realms. Right now, there is a world in the unseen realm just as real as the world in which you live filled with departed saints and other divine beings who are just as real as the people who fill the earth.

The Bible often speaks of God's divine family with the Hebrew word Elohim. On some occasions, this word is used to refer to God. Other times, it refers to the divine family as well as other fallen and demonic spirit beings. It is a general word for spiritual beings in the unseen realm, which can include God, the members of God's divine council, angelic and demonic beings at work in the world, and more. One example is found in Psalm 82:1, which says, "God [Elohim] has taken his place in the divine council; in the midst of the gods [Elohim] he holds judgment."

God's human and divine families in the seen and unseen realm meet at the Divine Council throughout the Bible.

The Divine Council is referred to throughout the Bible as "the assembly of the holy ones," "the council of the holy ones," "hosts," "the seat of the gods," "the mount of assembly," "the court...in judgment," and "the heavenly host."[g] The Bible gives us a clue that God has convened the divine assembly when He is revealed sitting on His throne. We get this same picture from Isaiah, Daniel, and John. Each one was taken from this realm into the unseen realm and placed amid the divine

---

[a] John 6:1–14 [b] Acts 2:43 [c] Acts 6:8 [d] Acts 19:11 [e] Acts 16:16–18 [f] Acts 13:6–12 [g] Psalm 82:1; 89:4–8; Ezekiel 28:2; Isaiah 14:12–14; Daniel 7:9–10; Luke 2:13

council gathered around God enthroned.[a] Jacob also had a visit from God, angels, and the Divine Council. They came down a ladder to meet with him and he said to them, "How awesome is this place! This is none other than the house of God, and this is the gate of heaven."[b] Jacob then named that place Bethel, which means house of God, because it was at least temporarily the meeting place of God's Divine Council and the connecting place for the two realms and two families of God.

The Divine Council met on earth in the Garden of Eden. There, the two realms were united. Throughout Biblical history, God has chosen a place of connection between the realms that includes the Garden of Eden, Tabernacle, Temple, Jesus Christ, and now the Holy Spirit in the believer. In the opening chapters of Genesis, we see God meeting in Eden with his human family (Adam and Eve) and His divine family (cherubim angel along with Satan, the fallen, rebellious angel cast out of Heaven according to Revelation 12:7-12). This explains why Eve was not startled when the Serpent showed up in the Garden of Eden; it was the place where the two realms met and so this was not uncommon or unexpected.

God intended that His two families – human and divine – live and work together as one united family. Sin caused humanity to rebel against God and side with Satan and demons, separating us from God and angels. Sin separated the realms. Everything changed with Jesus defeating the demonic realm on the cross and reclaiming us as His people. At Pentecost, the two realms and families came together once again, as the divine council was present at Pentecost. When we read of wind and fire in Acts 2 on the day of Pentecost, we are seeing the divine family appear with God's human family to again reunite the seen and unseen realms under the Lord of both, Jesus Christ.

Today, the Church in one realm is created by the Kingdom in the other realm. It serves as the outpost for the Kingdom, exists to witness to the Kingdom, and is the beginning of the unveiling of God's Kingdom across all creation. Starting at Pentecost, God intended that both His families would work together through the Church until they were forever together as one united, forever family.

The Bible uses the words "sign" and "wonder" to denote miracles, and these two words often appear together. Sometimes the New Testament also uses the word "power" to denote God showing up in a supernatural way to do something incredible. Curiously, even though Jesus Christ said that John the Baptizer is the

---

[a] Isaiah 6:1–6; Daniel 7:9–10; Revelation 4 [b] Genesis 28:10–22

greatest mere mortal to walk the planet[a], there was no miracle in John's ministry.[b] Furthermore, Jesus was clear that some people would not convert even if they saw a miracle with their own eyes.[c]

Miracles are what happens when the divine family visits the human family, and the Kingdom shows up and shows off in our world. These occasions are foretastes and foreshadowing of what is to come upon the return of King Jesus as ruler over both realms.

This is our tension – we are already citizens of the Kingdom, but not yet residents of the Kingdom. Some Christians relieve this tension with something called an *under-realized eschatology*. The big idea is that the Kingdom exists in Heaven and does not show up until it comes with King Jesus. Therefore, we should not expect much in the way of the supernatural or miraculous, such as healing.

Other Christians relieve this tension with something called *over-realized eschatology*. Those big words mean some believers think that since our citizenship is in Heaven, all of the power and prosperity of our eternal Kingdom life is ours to enjoy in this life. Both of Paul's letters to the Thessalonians were written to Christians who erred in this way, telling them that the work of God was not completed until Jesus returned a second time and the dead were raised.

Theologians refer to this tension with the language of *already*, but *not yet*. The Kingdom of God has already begun but is not yet completed.

Western Christians have seen Revelation as a book about future things (eschatology). They focus on the earthly scenes. Eastern Christians have seen Revelation as a book about worship (doxology). They focus on the Heavenly scenes. Both are true. Today God is being worshipped on Heaven and earth. One day, Heaven will come to earth, and God will be worshipped on earth as He is in Heaven. This is why one of the major themes of Revelation is "Worship God"; the book opens with John worshipping Jesus in the spirit and closes with a command to worship God until Jesus returns. When God's family gathers in the seen realm to worship, our prayers and praise rise into the unseen realm and join with God's family there. In Revelation, prayer and praise of God's people gathered in worship is depicted as "incense" that rises into the unseen realm and presence of God.[d] This might explain why, in corporate worship, there are often supernatural breakthroughs in people's lives, as in those gatherings, the families in the unseen and seen realms are united

---

[a] Luke 7:28 [b] John 10:41 [c] John 4:48 [d] Revelation 5:8, 8:3-4

in a supernatural way by the Holy Spirit.

<u>Do you have this gift?</u>

1. Do you truly believe that God can do the impossible?
2. When you read of the many miracles in the Bible, are you encouraged because you love to see God made known in ways that cannot be ignored?
3. Have you seen someone freed from demonic oppression?
4. Have you seen God perform miracles?
5. When you hear of or see miracles, is your faith in God greatly increased?
6. Do you use stories of God's miracles to help prove to others that Jesus is God?
7. Do you find God does supernatural things through your times of prayer and worship?
8. Does the Kingdom of God mean a great deal to you and serve as a driving motivator for all of your beliefs and behaviors?

Healing

<u>Place in Scripture:</u> 1 Corinthians 12:9

<u>Defined:</u> The gift of healing is the ability to call on God to heal the sick through supernatural means for the purpose of revealing God and His Kingdom where all sickness will be forever healed.

<u>General makeup:</u> Those with the gift of healing trust that God can heal the sick and pray in faith for the physical restoration of those in need. These people see healing as a sign that God uses to reveal His power to people so that many will come to believe in Jesus. People with this gift do not see someone healed every time they ask God, since healing is something that God alone decides to do.[a]

<u>Seen in Jesus' ministry:</u> Matthew 4:23–24 and 9:35 speak of Jesus' many healings.

<u>Illustrated biblically:</u> The Twelve had the gift of healing[b], as did the Seventy[c], Peter[d], and Paul.[e] Additionally, church leaders are supposed to pray for the sick so that God might heal them.[f]

<u>Healing theologically:</u>

God made you as one person in two parts. Part of you is immaterial and spiritual – your soul. Part of you is material and physical – your body. You are one

---

[a] e.g., Galatians 4:13–14; Philippians 2:27; 1 Timothy 5:23; 2 Timothy 4:20 [b] Matthew 10:1 [c] Luke 10:8–9 [d] Acts 5:14–16 [e] Acts 3:1–8 [f] James 5:13–16

whole person, and your spiritual and physical aspects affect one another. It is the same for all of us: sin has infected and affected every dimension of who we are. Sin has brought suffering to the body. Every one of us is either battling an injury or illness or walking with someone who is, which explains the enormous health care and pharmaceutical industry that exists to deal with the effects of the curse on our bodies.

Thankfully the God who made us also sent His Son to heal us, both body and soul, with outer and inner healing. Isaiah 53:5 says, "He was pierced for our transgressions; he was crushed for our iniquities; upon him was the chastisement that brought us peace, and with his wounds we are healed." Jesus died for both our sin and our suffering. Importantly, this promise of physical healing does not come with a time frame. Some of God's people will experience bodily healing in this life; all of God's people will experience total healing in their resurrection bodies in the eternal life.

Many times in Jesus' ministry, people were healed through deliverance. The demon brought the sickness or injury, and once the demon was gone, so was the sickness.[a]

A doctor named Luke wrote more of the New Testament than anyone. His concurring books, Luke and Acts, record verified healings by the Holy Spirit's power operating through Christ and Christians. Luke was also the personal physician to Paul and traveled on various mission trips, bandaging him up after his beatings, riots, or imprisonments. Paul and Luke had a close friendship and ministry partnership. Setting an example for all Christians and caregivers, Paul had a doctor who cared for his body and soul: "Luke the beloved physician."[b]

God can and does heal. Sometimes God does this naturally through a physician. Sometimes God does this supernaturally as the Great Physician. Therefore, healing does not replace traditional medicine. As we see in Doctor Luke, it is biblical to believe in both medical science and faith-filled prayer. We know many medical professionals who went to college for a degree and also go to the Spirit for power. They minister to not only the bodies of their patients but also their souls. This is the example of Doctor Luke, which helps prevent the either/or thinking that someone needs to be healed either only through prayer or only through a doctor.

Jesus began His public ministry reading from Isaiah 61: "The Spirit of the Lord

---

[a] Matthew 4:23–25; 8:16; 9:32–33; 12:22–23 [b] Colossians 4:14

is upon me, because he has anointed me to proclaim good news to the poor. He has sent me to proclaim liberty to the captives and recovering of sight to the blind, to set at liberty those who are oppressed, to proclaim the year of the Lord's favor".[a]

To begin with, Jesus was healed. He suffered and died on the cross and then rose to conquer sin, sickness, and death. When Jesus rose from death, some dead people also rose as a foreshadowing of the healing power of God's Kingdom. Jesus also healed others. Roughly 27 times in the Gospels, we see Jesus heal an individual. Roughly 10 times, we see Jesus heal entire groups of people.[b] Jesus performed other verified healings not recorded in the Bible.[c] Specific deliverance miracles Jesus performed through the Holy Spirit include healings from bleeding, epilepsy, deafness, muteness, and blindness.[d]

Once Jesus returned to Heaven following His healing from death, some wondered if God would continue to heal people. Doctor Luke wrote his follow-up book, Acts, which reports the supernatural acts of the Holy Spirit through Christians who continued the Spirit-filled ministry of Christ. Just as the Holy Spirit descended upon Christ at His baptism, the Holy Spirit then descended upon Christians so that they could live by His power and continue His kingdom ministry.

The Book of Acts records roughly 14 healing miracles. 12 of the 28 chapters in Acts record a miraculous healing reported by Doctor Luke. This was to be expected as it's what Jesus promised His first followers in Matthew 10:8, "Heal the sick, raise the dead, cleanse lepers, cast out demons." In obedience, we read of the early church in Acts 8:4-8, "Now those who were scattered went about preaching the word. Philip went down to the city of Samaria and proclaimed to them the Christ... they heard him and saw the signs that he did. For unclean spirits, crying out with a loud voice, came out of many who had them, and many who were paralyzed or lame were healed. So there was much joy in that city."

Simply stated, the miraculous is part of ministry. However, because God is free, we cannot make Him heal. Some say that by walking in faith and not sinning that no Christian needs to ever be sick, but Epaphroditus[e], Timothy[f], Trophimus[g], and Paul[h] each had sickness that was not healed despite the fact they deeply loved God and walked with Jesus faithfully.

---

[a] Luke 4:18–19 [b] Matthew 4:23–25; 8:16; 12:15; 14:14, 34–36; 15:30; 19:2; 21:14; Luke 6:17–19 [c] John 20:30 [d] Luke 13:11–16; Matthew 17:14–18; Mark 7:35; Matthew 9:22–23; 12:22 [e] Philippians 2:25–27 [f] 1 Timothy 5:23 [g] 2 Timothy 4:20 [h] 1 Corinthians 2:3; 2 Corinthians 11:30; 12:5, 7–10; Galatians 4:13

Every Christian will be fully, totally, completely, and eternally healed forever. This will happen upon the second coming of Jesus Christ and the resurrection of the dead. On that day, Revelation 21:4 says the curse will be fully lifted, death will be defeated, and Jesus "will wipe away every tear from their eyes, and death shall be no more, neither shall there be mourning, nor crying, nor pain anymore, for the former things have passed away."

Until the day of Jesus' return, the resurrection of the dead, removal of the curse, ruin of Satan and demons, and re-creation of the world, we are in the time between the times. The kingdom of God does show up in power at times, bringing revivals, awakenings, healings, and outpourings of God's presence that are sneak previews, glimpses, and dress rehearsals for the coming of King Jesus and the Kingdom of God. Until that day of sight, the righteous live by faith that all healing is coming for all of God's children.

Do you have this gift?

1. Do you have a deep compassion for people who are sick?
2. Do you have a deep conviction that God can heal anyone He chooses?
3. Do you enjoy praying for people who are sick, whether that be from a distance or up close through the laying on of hands?
4. Do you have an interest in medicine and finding ways to help people be most physically healthy?
5. Have you seen God heal someone?
6. When God heals someone, are you excited because it helps to reveal His power to others?
7. Do you long for the coming of God's Kingdom when there will be an end to all sickness since sin and its effects will be no more?
8. How have you seen signs and wonders follow you as you follow God?

Prophets/Prophecy

Place in Scripture: I Corinthians 12:28; Ephesians 4:11

Defined: Like a mail delivery person who does not write or edit the mail, but collects and delivers it, the prophetic calling combined two ministries. First, prophets received specific revelation directly from God. Second, they speak that revealed Word to the people God had called them to with the expectation of an obedient response to God. Prophets communicate their God-given message either by speaking or in writing.

<u>General makeup:</u> People with a prophetic gifting more easily spot compromise, sin and error and desire immediate change and action for Christ. They tend to be bold, sensitive to sin, and place a very high value on biblical behavior and telling the truth no matter the cost.

<u>Seen in Jesus' ministry:</u> Jesus was the prophet like Moses that was promised.[a] Jesus said He was a prophet without honor in His hometown[b], but that many people in the crowds who came to hear Him believed He was a prophet.[c]

<u>Illustrated biblically:</u> Roughly 25% of the Bible is prophetic in nature in that it tells us future details that God promises will happen. There is an entire genre of biblical literature called the "prophets" that includes both major (Isaiah, Jeremiah, Lamentations, Ezekiel, and Daniel) and minor prophets (Hosea, Joel, Amos, Obadiah, Jonah, Micah, Nahum, Habakkuk, Zephaniah, Haggai, Zechariah, and Malachi). John the Baptist[d], along with Judas and Silas[e] and John[f] all have this gift in the New Testament. There are times where the Holy Spirit falls on the church and numerous people prophesy.[g]

<u>Prophecy theologically:</u>

There is some and confusion about the gift of prophecy. Much like the spiritual gift of apostleship, there is both an office that is limited to a few people as Prophets and a gifting and ministry that is open to many who receive the spiritual gift of prophecy.

In the Old Testament, the title "prophet" refers to the office of the person chosen by God to both hear from and communicate for Him[h]. The prophets were also painfully aware of the weightiness of their call since they consciously knew that they were the very mouth of Almighty God and spoke for God Himself. This is clearly seen in Moses[i], Isaiah[k], Jeremiah[m], Amos[n], and Zechariah.[o] According to the Old Testament scholar Gerhard von Rad, the phrase "the word of Yahweh" appears 241 times in the Old Testament, 221 in relation to a prophet.

Additionally, Jesus[p], Paul[q] and John[r] all promised that false prophets would come. False prophets falsely claim to speak for God[s] and may also perform false miracles.[t]

---

[a] Deuteronomy 18; Acts 3:22, 7:37 [b] Mark 6:4-6 [c] Matthew 16:14, 21:11, 21:46 [d] Matthew 11:7-11 [e] Acts 15:32 [f] Revelation [g] Acts 19:6 [h] 1 Samuel 3:20; 1 Kings 18:36; 2 Kings 6:12; Haggai 1:1; Zechariah 1:1 [i] Exodus 4:16; 7:1–2 [k] Isaiah 1:20 [m] Jeremiah 1:7 [n] Amos 3:8; 7:16 [o] Zechariah 7:12 [p] Matthew 7:15; 24:11, 24 [q] Acts 20:29–31 [r] 1 John 4:1 [s] 1 Kings 22 [t] Deuteronomy 13:1–3; 2 Thessalonians 2:9; Revelation 13:13–15).

2 Peter 2:1-9 says, "False prophets also arose among the people, just as there will be false teachers among you, who will secretly bring in destructive heresies, even denying the Master who bought them, bringing upon themselves swift destruction. And many will follow their sensuality, and because of them the way of truth will be blasphemed. And in their greed they will exploit you with false words.... For if God did not spare angels when they sinned, but cast them into hell and committed them to chains of gloomy darkness to be kept until the judgment...then the Lord knows how to rescue the godly from trials, and to keep the unrighteous under punishment until the day of judgment."

The primary job of a true prophet is to prepare God's people for the real future. God knows and rules the future, and at times He chooses to reveal it to His people so they can prepare for it. Here are five key ways to recognize false prophets.

One, false prophets are wolves who lie about the future.[a] Sometimes false prophets prophesy that good times are coming when they are not. God says that false prophets "have misled my people, saying, 'Peace,' when there is no peace."[b] False prophets only say things people want to hear, ignore personal sin, and like to say that everyone is going to Heaven. Of false prophets we are told, "Woe to those who call evil good and good evil, who put darkness for light and light for darkness, who put bitter for sweet and sweet for bitter!"[c]

Two, false prophets prey on people's fears. Some people worry about a catastrophic future and are susceptible to scare tactics from wolves disguised as prophets. Sometimes wolves cause people to distrust everyone but them, and they rule out of fear and control. Jesus warns that "many false prophets will arise and lead many astray."[d]

Three, false prophets are often flatterers. They puff people up with praise, only saying what people want to hear rather than what God wants said. Jesus warns, "Woe to you, when all people speak well of you, for so their fathers did to the false prophets."[e] As demonic deception increases in the last days, "the time is coming when people will not endure sound teaching, but having itching ears they will accumulate for themselves teachers to suit their own passions, and will turn away from listening to the truth and wander off into myths."[f]

Four, false prophets often work with demonic power that makes them seem

---

[a] Matthew 7:15 [b] Jeremiah 6:14 [c] Isaiah 5:20 [d] Matthew 24:11 [e] Luke 6:26 [f] 2 Timothy 4:3-4

like God's anointed. Counterfeiting the kingdom of God, they lead people astray with clairvoyance, healing, revelations, visions, and other demonstrations of unusual supernatural power. But it is all demonic. "For false christs and false prophets will arise and perform great signs and wonders, so as to lead astray, if possible, even the elect."[a]

Five, false prophets are wolves who wear the sheep's clothing until the Good Shepherd, Jesus Christ, exposes them. Sometimes these people claim to love Jesus, prophesy at church, cast out demons, and see people they anoint with oil healed. But they have no relationship with the Shepherd because they are not among the sheep. "Not everyone who says to me, 'Lord, Lord,' will enter the kingdom of heaven...On that day many will say to me, 'Lord, Lord, did we not prophesy in your name, and cast out demons in your name, and do many mighty works in your name?' And then will I declare to them, 'I never knew you; depart from me, you workers of lawlessness.'"[b]

Despite false prophets and false prophecies, we are not to despise them but rather discern them. 1 Thessalonians 5:9-21 says, "Do not quench the Spirit. Do not despise prophecies, but test everything; hold fast what is good."

While no one single test for authentication of a prophet is appropriate, a few criteria help distinguish between true and false prophets. A true prophet had outstanding moral character[c], while false prophets did not.[d]. The prophecy of a true prophet came true every time.[e] False prophets were for hire and preached what they were paid to preach.[f] False prophets prophesied only peace.[g] The message of a false prophet conflicted with God's prior revelation, led to the worship of false gods, and was punishable by death.[h] Perhaps the most thorough descriptions of false prophets are given in Deuteronomy 18:14-22 and Jeremiah 23:9-40.

Today, Christians can also help to discern between true and false prophets by their inward testimony of the Spirit.[i] Prophecy is also spoken of in various ways throughout Scripture. Importantly, the New Testament does not elevate prophecy to the highest level of authority as the Old Testament does. Each potential prophecy is supposed to be tested and approved by church leaders.[k]

In the broadest sense, prophecy is sometimes the teaching ministry of

---

[a] Matthew 24:24 [b] Matthew 7:21-23 [c] Ezekiel 13:10–16 [d] Isaiah 28:7 [e] Deuteronomy 18; Jeremiah 28; 1 Kings 22 [f] Micah 3:11 [g] Jeremiah 6:13–14; 8:10–11 [h] Deuteronomy 13 [i] Deuteronomy 18:14–22; John 7:17 [k] 1 Corinthians 14:29–32; 1 Thessalonians 5:19–22

preaching the Bible as God's Word in the church. Examples include 1 Corinthians 14:4 where prophecy "edifies the church," 14:6–7 where Paul links prophecy and teaching, saying, "prophecy or word of instruction," and 14:24–25 where he explains that, through the Spirit-enabled preaching of the Bible, non-Christians will be convicted of their sin and give their lives to Jesus.

Prophecy is sometimes a revelation about a future event that God intends to reveal to the entire Church; a revelation that is authenticated by coming true as predicted. This is what Paul speaks of in 1 Corinthians 14:6 where he links "revelation or knowledge or prophecy." A clear example of this is Acts 11:28–29 where the prophet Agabus predicted a famine, thereby preparing the early Christians to better help people.

Prophecy is sometimes a word from God to be given to an individual. An example of this is the prophet Agabus who told Paul how he would die in Acts 21:10–11.

In summary, prophecy is a Holy Spirit enabled ministry to either:
1. Predict, or foretell future events to prepare people
2. Admonish or rebuke behavior to purify people. These prophecies in the Bible are often referred to as the "woes" because they often begin with the prophetic warning from God, "woe".

Do you have this gift?
1. Would you rather speak God's Word to others without much explanation than taking time to explain every detail?
2. When you see sin or errors do you feel compelled to confront them?
3. Do you tend to see more evil, sin and error than others?
4. Are you capable of detecting and refuting false teachings?
5. Are you bold for Christ?
6. Do you sometimes need to not just tell the truth, but do so in love?
7. Do you get frustrated when people are not obeying God or have no urgency about obeying Him?
8. Do others consider you more of a truth person than a love person and a justice person than a mercy person?

Tongues
Place in Scripture: 1 Corinthians 12:10, 12:28-30, 13:1, 14:1, 14:5-6, 14:18-23, 14:39
Defined: The word "tongues" is best translated "languages" from the Greek, so

speaking in tongues is a supernatural ability to pray in the Spirit in the language of Heaven, or speak to others in their native language, which is unknown to the speaker.

General makeup: This gift may also include the general ability to skillfully translate from one language to another as scholars do to get God's Word out in thousands of languages so that people can read God's Word in their own tongue/language. Additionally, this gift may include the ability of some Bible scholars to work masterfully from the original languages of the Bible (Hebrew, Greek Aramaic) to accurately help us learn the exact meaning of the Scriptures from the original languages and earliest manuscripts.

Seen in Jesus' ministry: Jesus is said to have perfectly operated in every spiritual gift listed in the Bible, with one curious exception, speaking in tongues. The debate over such things as speaking in tongues is important, but not of the utmost importance. Jesus is the perfect example of living a Spirit-filled life. We do not, however, know if Jesus ever spoke in tongues. The Bible is simply silent. I take this to mean that whether you speak in tongues or not, you can live a Spirit-filled life like Jesus, marked by godly character and a love for the Word of God.

Illustrated biblically: The spiritual gift of tongues, when listed among the various spiritual gifts lists that we have studied in this book, is always listed last. Some have taken this to mean that it is the least of the spiritual gifts, which may or may not be the case. Nonetheless, Paul said in 1 Corinthians 14:18, "I thank God that I speak in tongues more than all of you." He also said that when done publicly like in a church service, this gift needed to be utilized in such a way "so that the church may be built up" and others "benefit"[a]. For this to happen, we must not "forbid speaking in tongues"[b]. Instead, unlike private worship, when we are worshipping in public, we need to gather in a way that is "done decently and in order"[c]. The rest of 1 Corinthians 14 speaks to gathered public church meetings with parameters for tongues such as two or three people at the most, in an orderly fashion, with a person who can interpret so that everyone present can be edified[d]. Lastly, not every believer will receive the gift of tongues any more than every believer will receive the gift of administration[e] even though there are occasions where the Holy Spirit does decide to give the gift of tongues to everyone present.[f]

---

[a]1 Corinthians 14:5-6 [b]1 Corinthians 14:39 [c]1 Corinthians 14:40 [d]1 Corinthians 14:26-32, 39-40 [e]1 Corinthians 12:8-12, 12:29-30 [f]Acts 2:4

Tongues theologically:

One of the first things we learn about God in Genesis is that God speaks. Human beings communicate in languages because we were made in God's image.

Scholars tell us that there are around 7,000 languages that we know about on the earth today, in addition to the languages we simply do not know about. The Bible tells us in Genesis 11:1 that there was once a day when, "the whole earth had one language and the same words." The one language allowed ideology and frame of reference so that everyone could work together in a united way.

The problem is that, once sin entered the world, the unity that God provided could be used for sin and evil. This is precisely what happened in the rest of Genesis 11, which occurred in what is ancient Babylon and roughly the same location as present-day Iraq. As people kept moving further East, which is away from God[a], they devised a plan to build a counterfeit kingdom of God called Babel with a tower at the center so they could replace God and sit above to look down on the kingdom they made with their own hands. God came down to investigate this unified attempt to dethrone Him. Genesis 11:6-9 reports, "And the Lord said, 'Behold, they are one people, and they have all one language, and this is only the beginning of what they will do. And nothing that they propose to do will now be impossible for them. Come, let us go down and there confuse their language, so that they may not understand one another's speech.' So the Lord dispersed them from there over the face of all the earth, and they left off building the city. Therefore, its name was called Babel, because there the Lord confused the language of all the earth. And from there the Lord dispersed them over the face of all the earth."

The reversal of Babylon occurred at Pentecost in Acts 2:1-11. Following the resurrection of Jesus Christ from the dead, the Holy Spirit fell on people, and we read, "When the day of Pentecost arrived, they were all together in one place. And suddenly there came from heaven a sound like a mighty rushing wind, and it filled the entire house where they were sitting. And divided tongues as of fire appeared to them and rested on each one of them. And they were all filled with the Holy Spirit and began to speak in other tongues as the Spirit gave them utterance. Now there were dwelling in Jerusalem Jews, devout men from every nation under heaven. And at this sound the multitude came together, and they were bewildered, because each one was hearing them speak in his own language. And they were

---

[a] Genesis 11:2

amazed and astonished, saying, 'Are not all these who are speaking Galileans? And how is it that we hear, each of us in his own native language? Parthians and Medes and Elamites and residents of Mesopotamia, Judea and Cappadocia, Pontus and Asia, Phrygia and Pamphylia, Egypt and the parts of Libya belonging to Cyrene, and visitors from Rome, both Jews and proselytes, Cretans and Arabians—we hear them telling in our own tongues the mighty works of God.' And all were amazed and perplexed..."

At Pentecost, the unseen realm showed up in the seen realm so that God's family, both divine and human beings, were reunited as a sign pointing to the Kingdom of God where all the nations will be united under the Lordship of Jesus Christ. One day, all the nations of the earth will be no more but saved people from every nation will gather around Jesus Christ as the center of our lives, world, and history. Revelation 7:9 says, "After this I looked, and behold, a great multitude that no one could number, from every nation, from all tribes and peoples and languages, standing before the throne and before the Lamb, clothed in white robes, with palm branches in their hands, and crying out with a loud voice, 'Salvation belongs to our God who sits on the throne, and to the Lamb!'"

Until the Kingdom of God where we all speak the same language, or at least can understand and interpret all the languages of the nations (the spiritual gift of interpretation of tongues), we translate the Bible and other Christian books and songs into various languages as the Church is the greatest force for written languages and translation in world history. Furthermore, some Christians do have the supernatural spiritual gift of tongues. The confusion regarding tongues is that at least three different uses of the gift are mentioned in Scripture, as well as differing original Greek words that are all translated into English as "tongues".

One, tongues is a private prayer language. Paul speaks of this in 1 Corinthians 14:14 saying, "I pray in a tongue." This private prayer language may be the language of the angels in Heaven. Perhaps, just like various nations have a language, so too God's Kingdom has a language. This is what I believe Paul refers to saying in 1 Corinthians 13:1, "If I speak in the tongues of men and of angels, but have not love, I am a noisy gong or a clanging cymbal." The purpose of this private prayer language is to connect at the soul level with God, transferring burdens, and being encouraged by meeting with God in private. 1 Corinthians 14:2 says, "one who speaks in a tongue speaks not to men but to God; for no one understands him, but he utters mysteries in the Spirit." Praying privately in the Heavenly language of tongues is to be done to build up the individual believer in the same way that private Bible reading, and prayer, accomplish the same purpose. Paul says this very thing in 1 Corinthians 14:4, "The one who speaks in a tongue builds up himself..." However, there is a difference as we learned earlier in this book between our private and public worship. When we "come together" we need to consider others and what "builds them up" so that we are serving and not being selfish (this is the entire focus of 1 Corinthians 14).

Two, tongues is a missionary gift that enables someone to speak the gospel of Jesus to foreigners in their native language that the speaker does not know. Acts 2:1-13 records such an occasion when 3,000 people were saved in a day as the Gospel was preached through the early Christians. The original Greek text indicates that they not only heard the Gospel in their native language, but also their specific dialect. A modern-day example would be someone who only knew Hebrew suddenly, supernaturally, and extemporaneously speaking to a crowd of English speakers from the United States, Great Britain, India, and Scotland who all hear it with their particular dialect. Another example includes the Gentile coverts at Cornelius' house who had the same experience as Acts 2:1-13 in Acts 10:44-47 and 11:15-8. As an aside, some scholars will argue that since the hearers heard the gospel in their own language[a] in Acts, tongues may be more of a hearing gift for the listener than a speaking gift for the communicator. Either way, there is a supernatural work of God the Holy Spirit that overcomes the language barrier to reach a lost person.

Three, tongues is a revelatory language whereby a message of God is spoken in a language unknown to the speaker that must be translated into the native language of the people in the church so that they can understand what is being said. This use of tongues, therefore, also requires the assistance of someone with the gift of interpretation.[b] In this form, tongues functions a bit like both tongues and prophecy as something is revealed from God in one language, but needs to be translated into another.

Do you have this gift?

1. Do you have a private prayer language of tongues?
2. Are there times in your private prayer that you communicate at a soul level too deep for words that unburdens you and unlocks spiritual growth?
3. Have you ever had a prophetic word that was given through you in a language that was foreign to you?

_____

[a] Acts 2:6 [b] 1 Cor. 12:10, 14:27-28

4. Have you ever interpreted the prophetic word given through another person in a language that was foreign to you?

5. Do you have an ability to learn and master languages more easily than most people?

6. Do things like Bible translation and getting Bible teaching out in multiple languages to reach people from as many nations as possible matter a great deal to you?

7. Are you burdened for multicultural ministry, global missions, and reaching the nations for Christ?

A CLOSING PRAYER

As a Bible teaching pastor, it means the world to me that you would give me the honor of helping you study these great themes of the Bible, around which sometimes there is great confusion. I genuinely pray that you have a better idea of divine design, and that God leads you to a place where you can use your gifts for God's glory, others' good, and your joy.

Lastly, I pray that as you studied these great themes of spiritual gifts, two things would happen. One, I pray that your concept of God got bigger. He is more profound and powerful, more creative and considerate, and more free and faithful than we could ever hope or imagine. When Jesus told Nicodemus that the work of God was like a powerful wind, what He meant was that the work of the Spirit is powerful, unpredictable, and uncontrollable but altogether wonderful. Two, I pray that as we studied together that you would not only come to a better, deeper, and richer understanding of who God is, and who you are, but also how others are. If you are married, parenting a child, or serving in a ministry then you are interacting with precious people who are very different than you. The differences between your divine design and theirs should not be a point of contention, but cooperation. God made you differently because you are better together and by appreciating one another, encouraging one another, and serving one another, the Kingdom of God will be strengthened, and your relationship will be deepened! Lastly, if you'd like to share what you've learned with us, what ministry God is leading you do, or how we can pray for you, please go to realfaith.com and let us know. There, you can find the free sermon series along with free daily devotions that correspond with this sermon series along with a growing mountain of free Bible teaching made possible by our generous ministry partners. We'd love to serve you, pray for you, and hear from you!

NOTES

1. Christopher Zoccali, "Spiritual Gifts," ed. John D. Barry et al., The Lexham Bible Dictionary (Bellingham, WA: Lexham Press, 2016.
2. R. P. Spittler, "Spiritual Gifts," ed. Geoffrey W. Bromiley, The International Standard Bible Encyclopedia, Revised (Wm. B. Eerdmans, 1979–1988), 603.
3, Donald W. Mills, "Blasphemy," ed. John D. Barry et al., The Lexham Bible Dictionary (Bellingham, WA: Lexham Press, 2016).

MARK DRISCOLL & REAL FAITH

With Pastor Mark, it's all about Jesus! Mark and his wife Grace have been married and doing vocational ministry together since 1993. They also planted The Trinity Church with their five kids in Scottsdale, Arizona as a family ministry (thetrinitychurch.com) and started Real Faith, a ministry alongside their daughter Ashley that contains a mountain of Bible teaching from Pastor Mark as well as content for women, men, parents, pastors, leaders, Spanish-speakers, and more.

Pastor Mark has been named by *Preaching Magazine* one of the 25 most influential pastors of the past 25 years. He has a bachelor's degree in speech communication from the Edward R. Murrow College of Communication at Washington State University as well as a master's degree in exegetical theology from Western Seminary in Portland, Oregon. For free sermons, answers to questions, Bible teaching, and more, visit **RealFaith.com** or download the **Real Faith app**.

Together, Mark and Grace have authored "Win Your War" and "Real Marriage". Pastor Mark has authored numerous other books including "Spirit-Filled Jesus", "Who Do You Think You Are?", "Vintage Jesus", and "Doctrine". Pastor Mark and his daughter Ashley Chase have also written "Pray Like Jesus" as a father-daughter project.

If you have any prayer requests for us, questions for future Ask Pastor Mark or Dear Grace videos, or a testimony regarding how God has used this and other resources to help you learn God's Word, we would love to hear from you at **hello@realfaith.com**.